transition
to
nowhere

Vietnamese Refugees in America

Charter House Publishers Inc.

Nashville/London

by
William T. Liu

Maryanne Lamanna
Alice Murata

Copyright © 1979 by
Special Service for Groups/Asian American
Mental Health Research Center and
CHARTER HOUSE PUBLISHERS INC.
Nashville, Tennessee

Library of Congress Catalog Card Number 78-21129
ISBN 0-8202-0189-8

Manufactured in the United States of America

Sách này để riêng tặng
tất cả những người Việt tị nạn
mà chúng tôi đã được hân hạnh phỏng vấn
năm 1975 tại trại Pendleton

This book is dedicated to
all the Vietnamese refugees
whom we had the honor to interview
in 1975 at Camp Pendleton

Preface

When the news of the largest airlift of refugees came through the evening news, Mr. George Nishinaka, then Acting Director of the Asian American Mental Health Research Center, phoned me from Los Angeles. I had then already promised to assume the duties as Director of the Center at the end of the academic semester at Notre Dame. Mr. Nishinaka, a Nisei veteran of World War II, had spent time in a war relocation camp. He felt the decision to set up reception camps in various military installations created a situation too important to be ignored by mental health professionals. He asked me to come to California to take a look at the situation firsthand.

Working through the office of John Brademas, Congressman from the Third District in Indiana, and with Ambassador Dean Brown, a career diplomat appointed by the President to take charge of the entire refugee operation, I was able to receive permission to visit Camp Pendleton.

In order to accomplish the study of refugees at camp, several factors had to be present. First, the decision to act immediately, reflecting the decisiveness and flexibility of Mr. George Nishinaka as an administrator. Second, the recent funding of the Asian American Mental Health Research Center, with some money set aside for emergencies. Third, an invitation by Navy psychiatrists resulting from a conversation overheard in a hospital hallway by a Japanese American graduate student in anthropology. Fourth, availability of my time to devote to the immediate task before assuming duties as the Director of the Center. In retrospect, without any one of these four factors, none of the stories in the following pages could have been told.

In May, 1975, when the National Community Advisory Board of the Research Center convened in San Francisco, the question was raised as to whether or not the Board considered the monitoring of the adjustment of the newest Asian group in America to be a priority research project. More than two decades of military and political events in Indo-China had resulted in a large number of refugees who were, for the most part, only the high risk group of Vietnamese, Cambodians, and Laotians—those who had worked closely with the American diplomatic, military, and business organizations, and those who were relatives of American nationals. Later we discovered that hundreds upon thousands of refugees had come because they "followed the crowd" or "got picked up" during the last forty-eight hours before the fall of Saigon.

The Board quickly endorsed the idea of immediately mobilizing research resources since the refugee situation provided an excellent opportunity to begin research in the four priority areas already determined by the Board: Problems of the Elderly, Economic Conditions of Asian Americans, Immigration Problem, and Effects of Negative Stereotypes of Asians.

Many of the refugees involved three generations. These families faced a gradual "nuclearization" to gain conjugal independence because of the increasing pressure of the political, social, and economic systems of America. The pressure toward conjugal independence from larger kinship control undoubtedly will highlight the problems of the older generation. Since refugees had been uprooted from familiar surroundings, had lost their businesses, and, at least for a brief period, their skills and experience were not readily transferable to a new society, they experienced problems of employment. And this during a time when the United States had entered into a period of two-digit inflation rate as well as high unemployment. Refugees under these circumstances consequently were expected to face many of the same problems as other new immigrants—and more. Finally, Indo-Chinese, as other Asians in the United States, were judged by their neighbors as "Orientals," not to mention the effects of war propaganda influencing thousands of returning veterans.

For many, the violence and destruction of the two decades of conflict deeply scarred their lives. The final evacuation from a war-torn country may have ended the uncertainties for some but created many new uncertainties for others.

On our first visit to Camp Pendleton, the Marines were busy erecting tents, anticipating a large number of refugees. And my task was to determine how to begin monitoring the progress of the refugees' eventual integration into American society.

In June, Lt. Comm. Harold Ward of the Naval Health Research Unit of the Department of Navy called to ask if the newly established Asian American Mental Health Research Center would help the Navy to monitor the mental health conditions of refugees in Camp Pendleton. I then met with the head of the Stress Medicine Unit of that office, Captain Richard Rahe, who is well known for his research on life change and stresses, and Lt. Comm. John Looney, a child psychiatrist who was particularly concerned with the problems of the unaccompanied children in the camp. Through the Navy psychiatrists, I met and later worked closely with Dr. Tran Minh Tung, a member of the refugee group who was asked by Drs. Rahe and Ward to head a mental health clinic in the dispensary. In May, the Asian American Mental Health staff began to work on the interview schedule and sampling procedures. With the help of the Navy officers, the Research Center was able to make effective contributions as a part of the mental health monitoring unit in Camp Pendleton.

However, the rather smooth beginning was too good to last long. In July, the civilian authority in the camp decided to suspend the monitoring work of the staff of the Research Center. After several discussions and efforts at persuasion, mainly through the efforts of Dr. Tung and myself, we were able to resume our activities. The data collection activities continued until October. Toward the end of the year, the camp was closed in accordance with the schedule. The first phase of the refugee evacuation task officially ended.

Obviously, a task such as the one reported in this volume is the combined effort of many individuals whose contributions must be acknowledged. Drs. Richard Rahe and Harold Ward should be given all the credit they deserve for their initiation and design of the project and their vision to capture a moment in history which

CONTENTS

Introduction

There are understandable reasons why once the refugee is resettled he is more often than not equated by administrators and general public alike with the voluntary migrants around him. . . . First of all, the resettled refugee ceases to be a problem demanding international solution . . . he becomes a closed case for whom solution has been found. —Kunz, 1973

The process of becoming a refugee developed as a concern of striking immediacy in April, 1975, as South Vietnam fell to the Viet Cong. Approximately 145,000 Vietnamese fled the country, eventually arriving in the United States to be cared for temporarily in refugee camps. How to receive, care for, resettle, and cope with the problems of refugees became a focus of public and private attention and effort in this country.

Need for research on refugees.—This task was made most difficult by the lack of background information and understanding of refugee movements and problems. The unique emergency character of refugee flights tends to militate against the accumulation of practical expertise and intellectual understanding of refugee phenomena. We think of refugee movements as unpredictable and nonrepetitive events—hence a failure to systematically analyze and accumulate past experience for future use. The result is a lack of preparedness.

Yet, as Kunz points out:

"The past is prologue . . . Specialists appear to be too preoccupied with immediate service demands to take the time needed for reflection. And yet . . . the utility of a source book on the mental health needs of refugees would appear self-evident."

The military coordinator of Camp Pendleton stressed the need for the publication of a reference document:

"There was no reference material or documentation of any sort

1

on the subject available about the Base, nor were any Marines experienced in this type operation. With less than eighteen hours before the arrival of the first planeload of refugees . . . there was no time for research, lengthy discussion, or the normal staffing usually associated with a practical problem. A great deal of time and effort, that could have been directed to other aspects of the operation, was spent refining . . . the organization . . . and determining the kinds of facilities needed. . . . Initially, problems arose that were not anticipated, many of a recurring nature, that soon became obvious were endemic to any refugee operation. . . . While it is unlikely that another mass migration of refugees on the scale of operation "New Arrivals" would take place in the foreseeable future.—U.S. Marine Corps, 1975:43

In this comment, the need for guidance in the specific phase of refugee reception is perceived, but the words *while it is unlikely* set the refugee flight apart as a unique, atypical, and nonrecurring phenomenon. If, in fact, refugee movements are as they sometimes appear to us, *unique events*, there could not be a "process of becoming a refugee" but only a series of isolated events defying abstraction and generalization. Such a perception perhaps explains the sociological inattention to refugees.

There is also a tendency to get caught up, as in the case of Vietnam, with the political events leading to and the political implications of the refugee movement, so that a more intellectualized approach seems impossible and inappropriate. Yet, as Kunz points out:

"This calls for an organized body of advice for operational personnel and emphasizes the need to look at refugee situations not as individual historical occurrences, each distinctly different and circumscribed in its locus and time, but as recurring phenomena with identifiable and often identical sets of causalities bearing on selectivity of participation and flight patterns, all of which in the long run affect refugee outcomes."— Kunz, 1973:127

Earlier refugee movements.—Certainly, if we expand our space and time horizons, we find that refugee movements have occurred with considerable frequency in the mid-twentieth century. Since 1945, over forty-five million persons have been denied residence in their homelands either voluntarily or involuntarily for a variety of political and economic reasons (United Nations:

Refugee Report, 1969). In a sense, all refugees have the refugee experience as a common bond, but the actual experiences differ widely for individuals and groups. The 1944-46 and the 1948-52 refugees from Europe were largely Jewish in faith but racially indistinguishable from the European stock of the American population. The Cuban refugees of the early sixties had quite a different experience. They blended easily into some fifty thousand Cuban residents in the Miami area, even though a shortage of housing and other facilities did cause some problems. It is still too early to predict the course of events with respect to the Indo-Chinese refugees. Available facts already indicate, however, that the camp situation for the Vietnamese differed greatly from that of the Lake Oswego Camp used between August, 1944, and February, 1946.

Fort Ontario in Lake Oswego, New York, 1944-46.—On June 8, 1944, President Roosevelt sent a memorandum to the Secretaries of War, Navy, and Interior, the Director of the Budget, and the Executive Director of the War Refugee Board, outlining the division of responsibilities of each in connection with the selection and transportation of war refugees and administration of the shelter. A token of 1,000 refugees, mostly Jewish in faith, were brought to the United States. Under appropriate security restrictions, they remained for the duration of the war. A large proportion of the refugee population had better-than-average educations, and many had been successful business or professional people in their homelands.

The Fort Ontario group was fortunate in many ways. First, they were a small group compared to other refugee groups who came into the United States at different times. Second, most of the people living in communities surrounding the shelter were friendly and sympathetic. An advisory committee of town residents was formed and was most helpful to the refugees. More than two hundred refugee children attended the Oswego public and parochial schools. Their books and supplies were paid for by public and private organizations. The War Relocation Administration (WRA) provided grants for incidentals in addition to the essentials such as clothing, food, medical care, and adult education. During this period in the shelter, most men were employed in project duties at the rate of eighteen dollars per month. They took charge of their own mess halls and provided a major portion of the services in the hospital, personnel office, warehouses, shops, and sanitation. These refugees formed an Advisory council of shelter residents, elected on a basis of proportional nationality. In the fall of 1944, when help was needed at nearby fruit farms, more than fifty refugees were recruited for a number of weeks at the local wage scale.

The resettlement process was completed smoothly and rapidly by family or agency sponsorship. The shelter population, upon dispersal, spread to seventy communities in twenty-one states. The majority, however, were taken in by relatives mainly from the eastern seaboard states. Perhaps one of the ingredients for the successful resettlement was the fact that throughout the period of confinement, refugees were allowed to have contact with American society in some form. They were able to learn the English language and the workings of American systems. Their children were able to be a part of the town's school system. This is in contrast to the Vietnamese camps, where only minimal contact with American society was permitted, and where self-government generally was absent.

Cuban refugees in Miami, Florida.—Approximately 215,000 Cubans immigrated to the United States between the latter part of 1958 and the early part of 1963 (Martin, 1963), with an eventual total of 500,000 in all. Since authorities labeled Cuban immigrants as self-imposed political exiles rather than refugees to be resettled, no large scale detention shelters were set up to restrict the freedom of Cuban refugees (Fagen, Brody, and O'Leary, 1968). Of the 215,000 Cubans who came between the years of 1958 and 1963, fewer than 80 percent had registered with the Refugee Center in Miami. The remaining 20 percent of the refugees probably had more money, status, and connections. In any case, the Cuban immigrant differed from the average Cuban of the prerevolution Cuban census in occupation, education, and income. The selectivity of Cuban immigrants may well account for the relatively problem-free resettlement, but authorities also agreed that these refugees were absorbed by Miami's more than fifty thousand permanent Cuban residents who were able to provide volunteer agency assistance. The schools of Dade County and Miami also provided help, and universities offered teacher training so qualified Cuban teachers could accept the hundreds of openings in high schools and colleges for Spanish language teachers. The University of Miami offered medical refresher courses to hundreds of Cuban physicians to enable them to pass the examination of the Educational Council for Foreign Medical Graduates. All of these programs were needed, and, in retrospect, much of the initial help rendered to the highly skilled as well as less skilled workers during the early sixties may have been quite important to the successful adjustment of Cuban refugees.

The Ugandan Asian in Great Britain.—Within three months after the first Ugandan Asian arrived at London's Heathrow Airport in 1974, many more of the twenty-seven thousand-plus refugees reportedly expelled by President Idi Amin of Uganda followed. These Asian refugees were confronted with a sullen—even hostile—public reaction from the native people of Britain. The *London Sunday Telegraph* reported the public's highly critical reaction to the new immigrants:

"A further large swift influx of colored immigrants to Britain is wholly undesirable on social grounds . . . The Ugandan Emergency must affect our ability to take any further immigration for the foreseeable future. If there are complaints, let them be addressed to President Amin and the blame put squarely at the door of Black racialism."—Kuepper, Lackey and Swinerton, 1974: chapter 3, p. 1

Britain's first step was to set up resettlement centers to serve as a one- or two-day stopover in transit as refugees made their way into other British communities. The first camp opened was at Stradishall, a former military installation quite distant from major population centers. More than four thousand eventually arrived and were settled in sixteen camps. The original plan was for relatives and friends to "take care" of the refugees, but reality called for a custodial detention concept:

"By the time Rambhai Patel and his family arrived in late October, he recalled few being met by relatives; instead most were going to camps. This alarmed the Resettlement Board. Why had such a large number of Asians needed the camps in the first place, and why were they leaving at such a slow rate?"—Ibid., chapter 4, p. 5

Most of the camp administrators and their deputies were former military officers whose names were found on Britain's roster of executives available for employment. The camp administrators were responsible for the logistics of the centers—lodging, food, transportation, and the coordination of volunteer organizations providing services to the Asians. One of the most frequently mentioned problems was food. The refugees were fed in the military mess halls. The work of voluntary organizations was crucial in opening up the resettlement centers (camps) and later in performing many valuable services in their operation.

In the Kuepper, *et al* report (1974), two points were brought up in connection with the description of the atmosphere in these camps. The first had to do with the potential problem created by the variety of religious and sectarian groups the Asians brought with them from East Africa. The second was the potential hostility fostered by the political and military conflicts in the early seventies on the Indian subcontinent—a situation quite similar to the Vietnamese camps, though admittedly with some fundamental differences. For example, Buddhists and Christians in Vietnam did not have the hostile relationship which existed between Hindu and Muslim. Evidence indicates that a rather heterogeneous refugee population often contains different class and political ideologies as well as different life styles as was the case in the Vietnamese detention camps.

After leaving the camp, Ugandan Asian refugees tended to go to communities where there were other Asian residents. British authorities, in private planning, defined communities and sectors of communities in terms of "red" or "green" areas, depending on availability of housing, schools, social services, and employment. If two of the four factors were in short supply, the area would be designated a "red" area. Although it was not entirely clear whether the government had intended to disperse the refugees, the dichotomy of "green" and "red" areas structurally guaranteed a scattered resettlement. These were some of the ironies and problems of the British experience with the Ugandan Asian refugees in the early seventies. The designation of "green" and "red" areas in settlement was intended to ease the local burden. By doing so, however, a dispersion of the refugee population was accomplished, thus unintentionally depriving the refugee population of forming effective and close emotional and mutual-help bonds.

Factors of successful resettlement.—Over the last three to four decades, a large number of people in the world have been relocated because of political and military interventions. Unfortunately, the personal and societal consequences of migration under such aggravated circumstances mostly are unrecorded. We have little information on the Hungarian exodus of 1956, the mass movements of Hindus and Muslims at the beginning of statehood for both India and Pakistan, or the split between Pakistan and Bangladesh. Specific instances of refugee settlement with a transitional period of camp confinement may have unusual psychological and health impact on the refugees. This requires further research. Data on the World War II confinement of Japanese Americans and the Korean prisoners of war may help us to understand the impact of camp experience on mental and physical health, but such material is insufficient for us to assess the Vietnamese refugees' situation.

The three cases cited above, however, may be sufficient to point out certain factors associated with problematic adjustment of refugees. The first is the degree of refugee contact with the community during the transition period. In the case of the Cubans, unrestricted association with the community townspeople presented the least problem, in spite of the language barriers. For the Algerian immigrants housed in Fort Ontario, association with the community was made through work, school, and visitation. The Ugandan Asians in Britain who initially were isolated from the population center had a more difficult adjustment during confinement and the period immediately following discharge. A second factor is the community's reaction to the refugee population, with the inherent issue of race. The stigma of race, in addition to the experience of detention, compounds any attempts at successful resettlement.

Comparative analyses of the earlier Fort Ontario experience, the Hungarian refugee experience, and the experience of Ugandan Asian refugees in Britain provide additional insight into the problems of the race issue. For example, the Hungarians, about whom we have little recorded data in this regard, did not find themselves moving into ethnic neighborhoods populated with relatives or family friends. For the Hungarians, like the Vietnamese refugees in the United States, both their exodus and their final destination were functions of chance rather than of carefully made plans. More than one fourth of those Hungarians who migrated to Britain eventually made their way to Canada.

Without the barrier of race difference, Hungarians were absorbed into European and North American societies with remarkable speed and ease. On the other hand, the Asians' readily identifiable physical characteristics inevitably will impede their acceptance, in spite of many good-willed people who have expressed their wholehearted welcome of the Vietnamese refugees into their communities.

To illustrate this point, the experience of the Japanese Americans during World War II has been mentioned frequently in connection with the Vietnamese camp conditions. The War Relocation Authority (WRA) staff, from their special vantage point, could see that "with every passing week most camp residents were losing initiative and self-reliance, becoming progressively disaffected with and maladjusted to the larger American community . . . and (to many of the evacuees) the camps provided refuge from the storms of racial prejudice."—WRA, 1964:184.

The reception of evacuees who returned to the West Coast after the war was unfavorable. Many of the camp residents, as reported by WRA staff, "had pronounced tendency to exaggerate both the degree and scope of anti-evacuee sentiment outside and were also too strongly inclined to belittle or overlook the genuinely significant manifestations of growing good will and tolerance toward the group over wide areas of the country."—WRA, 1964:185

The refugee as a social type.—It is important to document the story of the Vietnamese refugee flight, reception, and resettlement, attempting as much as possible to analyze underlying processes and attitudes to contribute to a conceptual understanding of the refugee as a social psychological type whose movements are socially patterned. Kunz (1973) correctly asserts that concepts, definitions, and research designs on migrants and their adjustment in the host community must be clearly delineated and tested against the realities of the refugee situation. The Vietnamese refugee should be understood not only in terms of the unique historical events of 1975 but also as a case study of the process of becoming a refugee. This process must be seen from inside and out; that is, the refugee phenomena can be understood from the point of view of the refugee—the circumstances, actions, and possible decisions placing him in the refugee status initially—and in terms of (host) societal reaction.

Actually, "the refugee" should not be thought of as a fixed

status but as a career model with a time sequence and contingencies. The acute refugee (this typology from Kunz, to be discussed later) is not selective. The refugee's primary purpose is to reach a place that will assure him personal safety, without knowing much about what may lie ahead. For this reason, the course of migration and settlement may develop in several stages, each followed by a stochastic process of defining the situation and reassessing future possibilities. In the process of finding a satisfactory solution, each step in turn redefines the number of alternatives open to the refugee. As the process continues, new situations call for novel adaptions never before experienced by the newcomer. For the large group, new forms of group life may develop and creative social institutions may emerge which are drastically different from the old and familiar. When no solutions can be found, and when all adjustive strategies have failed, physical and mental health may suffer. Thus, the person enters the refugee status, follows a contingent career, and perhaps, at some point, leaves the status of refugee.

The refugee, from another point of view, is not an actor or reactor but is the object of attitudes and behavioral reactions of the receiving country or other authorities—in other words, a social problem. Entry and exit from the refugee status as well as career contingencies are affected by the efforts and definitions of the situation by representatives of the host society who have different entry and exit requirements for refugee status, and different time horizons for the adjustment process. The assumption that refugee status is clearly delineated, extremely temporary and transitory, and agreed upon by refugee and caretaker society is perhaps the popular view of the refugee phenomenon, but one which obscures many problems and divergences. One of the interesting features of the Vietnamese refugee resettlement experience is the apparent conflict over the attempt of the United States government to phase out the camps and withdraw from active concern with subsequent resettlement problems—an attempt, in essence, to quickly terminate refugee status. This was strongly objected to by some refugee spokesmen and advocates in the communities.

Scope of this book.—We will outline the initial creation or designation of refugees, from both the subjective (refugee) and objective (societal reaction) points of view and will follow the stages of the refugee career defined in terms of refugee movements: 1) flight, 2) transit, 3) sojourn in camp, 4) sponsorship out and subsequent immediate resettlement, 5) long-term adjustment (only speculative comment here). We will compare perspectives of the refugees and those of various segments of the receiving society: immediate bureaucracy, government, private agencies, and public opinion. There is conflict between the two perspectives on how matters should be handled within each career stage, and the points at which transition from one stage to another should occur. There appears to be a continual struggle over timing. Some refugees wish to prolong their refugee status because of their need for practical assistance and time to accept the reality and irreversibility of what has happened, as well as accepting the serious difficulties of readjustment. On the other hand, refugees charged with official responsibility (supported by the limited attention span of the general public) seem eager to move the refugees into the general population as rapidly as possible, thus discharging them as a social problem.

The prolongation of the refugee status never has been considered desirable from the viewpoint of the official governmental agencies. Refugee status means continual governmental assistance under public—often international—scrutinies. In the late summer of 1977, for example, when public pressures demanded an extension of the 1975 law on refugee relief for the Indo-Chinese in the United States, the extension was granted by the Congress without, at least initially, appropriation attached to the Act. The Interagency Task Force still maintained offices in the nation's capital. Like departing guests at the entrance foyer bidding goodbye to the hosts and to each other, the departure has taken two years and would be expected to take longer. The slowness in completing its tasks caused much anxiety and prompted Senator Edward Kennedy's Subcommittee on Immigration and Refugees to propose a bill to end the "parolee" status for Indo-Chinese refugees and to grant immediate resident status.

Throughout this book we will maintain a dual perspective from the refugees' and host society's points of view. Sometimes conflicting definitions of the situation are advanced. We will also present, maintain, and develop Kunz's distinction between the refugee and the voluntary migrant, employing Kunz's kinetic rather than motivational model of refugee movements (Kunz, 1973), exploring the five stages mentioned above.

1
The Flight from Vietnam

I saw everyone running to the harbor, so I decided to go along. —a refugee

A refugee, by definition, is displaced from his home country by events outside his control. Circumstances are such that it is no longer viable for the refugee to remain in his home country in his customary round of life, so he chooses to flee. In some cases, the refugee does not in any sense have a choice, because he is physically swept up in a panic exodus or caught outside his home country by the turn of events. Entry into refugee status thus, to some degree, is involuntary, and the refugee often is ill-prepared psychologically and practically for his sudden departure from his familiar social world. Ultimately, refugee status must also be validated by a country of destination which agrees to receive or to keep the involuntary migrant. Often tenure in a particular country, such as the United States, is difficult to obtain legally or difficult to reach geographically because of the great distance from Vietnam.

The fall of South Vietnam and evacuation plans.—An understanding of the last days of "free" Vietnam is necessary to establish a perspective for examining the Vietnamese refugees. As is well known, the military situation deteriorated rapidly for Thieu's government in April, 1975. By April 21, Thieu submitted his resignation as Prime Minister and was succeeded by the Vice Prime Minister, Huong. But political stability steadily worsened, corresponding to military setbacks. By April 27, Huong, in turn, transferred his authority to General (Big) Minh. Meanwhile, on

11

April 23, in the United States, President Ford conceded that the war in Indochina was finished "as far as America is concerned." This was the start of putting a massive rescue operation in action to salvage United States nationals in South Vietnam and "high risk" Vietnamese.

It was a mere three weeks from the earliest date of planning to the actual date on which evacuation was to take place in April, 1975. During this period, members of the Congress, the foreign service personnel in certain parts of the world, and at least twelve Federal agencies had been consulted and informed of pending evacuation plans. During the second week of April, State Department officials consulted with House and Senate Committees regarding the use of the Attorney General's "parole" authority for evacuees from Vietnam, Cambodia, and Laos. During the second and third weeks of the same month, the American mission in Geneva was asked to request assistance from United Nations agencies and other international organizations in locating third countries willing to accept refugees from Indochina. On April 18, President Ford created the Interagency Task Force (IATF) to coordinate activities concerning the evacuation of refugees from Vietnam and their subsequent resettlement problems. He appointed Ambassador L. Dean Brown as the Director of the Interagency Task Force to coordinate evacuation and relief efforts.

While United States Ambassador to South Vietnam Martin insisted that the evacuation programs be put off as late as strategically permissible out of concern for the panic that might subsequently arise throughout Saigon, the Defense Department already had mapped out four alternative plans for emergency evacuations.

The extent of the rescue effort in terms of categories of persons eligible steadily expanded. On April 14, parole was authorized for dependents of American citizens currently in Vietnam. On April 19, parole was extended to include the categories of relatives of American citizens or of permanent resident aliens who were petition holders. On April 22, the Interagency Task Force requested care and maintenance of 50,000 refugees for ninety days on the island of Guam. On April 25, the Attorney General authorized parole for additional categories of relatives, Cambodians in third countries, and up to fifty thousand "high-risk" Vietnamese, having announced on April 22 that regular immigration requirements would be waived to allow for the sanctuary of up to one hundred thirty thousand refugees from Indochina (seventy-five thousand relatives and fifty thousand high-risk persons) (U.S. Interagency Task Force, 1975b, Annex, p. 1).

"President Ford spoke of the safety of nearly 6,000 Americans who remained in South Vietnam, and tens of thousands of South Vietnamese employees of the United States Government, of news agencies, of contractors and businesses for many years whose lives, with their dependents, are in my opinion, in grave peril. There are tens of thousands of other South Vietnamese intellectuals, professors, teachers, editors, and opinion-leaders who have supported the South Vietnamese cause and the alliance with the United States, to whom we have a profound moral obligation."—U.S. Marine Corps, 1975: i-ii.

The evacuation.—The evacuation of Americans and Vietnamese from Saigon began on April 15 by commercial and military aircraft. Categories of persons evacuated included past and present United States government employees, officials whose cooperation was necessary for the evacuation of American citizens, individuals with knowledge of sensitive United States government intelligence operations, vulnerable political or intellectual figures, communist defectors, employees of United States firms operating in Vietnam, employees of voluntary agencies, certain labor officials, participants in United States government-sponsored programs, and a "catch-all" category of farmers, fishermen, students, street vendors, small shopkeepers, local policemen, military, and many others who did not meet the prescribed evacuation and parole guidelines. The records show the majority in this last category simply were caught up in the panic of the moment and joined the evacuation chain in order to escape the combat zone (U.S.M.C. 1975: ii).

The first wave of refugees, involving some ten thousand to fifteen thousand people, began at least a week or ten days before the collapse of the Thieu Government; a second wave of an estimated eighty-six thousand Vietnamese and Americans were evacuated by aircraft during the last days of April. At first about five thousand South Vietnamese and Americans were flown out of the country daily by commercial and military aircraft, but this scale of evacuation proved to be insufficient. By April 29, the situation deteriorated and Tan Son Nhut Airport became jammed with desperate Vietnamese trying to escape. "Operation Frequent Wind," the riskiest alternative plan but the only one feasible under the circumstances, was adopted by President Ford in conjunction with his National Security Council. The plan called for evacuation of the qualified personnel and their dependents by giant helicopters. According to Newsweek (May 12, 1975, p. 28), it was a "logistical success . . . the biggest helicopter lift of its kind in history." Much more desperate, heroic, albeit oftentimes unscrupulous, efforts were resorted to by individual Vietnamese. Those who had proper connections and financial resources had left for Clark Air Force Base in the Philippines. The less fortunate ones had to bribe their way through the security guards or force their entry onto the helicopters. *U.S. News* reported "some wealthy Vietnamese promised Americans large amounts of money to marry or adopt their children to insure safe evacuation from the Communist-threatened city. A few even offered their wives" (May 5, 1975, p. 19). Regardless of the motives of these refugees, one cannot help but admire their desperate attempts to reach freedom.

The third and last wave involved some forty to sixty thousand Vietnamese who left in small boats, ships, and commandeered aircraft and arrived at Subic Bay and Guam during the first two weeks in May after having been picked up, in many cases, by U.S. ships standing off the coast. These Vietnamese sailed daringly out to sea in various kinds of make-do vessels—just hoping they would be picked up.

Refugee flight—the refugees' perspective.—Some of the flavor of the flight experience can be captured from interviews with refugees conducted by the staff of the Asian American Mental Health Research Center in cooperation with the Navy Health Research Center (San Diego) at Camp Pendleton from early June through the closing weeks of the Camp in September 1975.

Interviews were conducted with fifty-nine heads of households, and with two hundred two respondents over thirteen years of age in those households. (See Appendix for details on sample, interview training, and procedure.) The interview schedules included standardized questions dealing with general demographic and socio-economic characteristics of the respondents. Other questions attempted to probe into the psychodynamic aspects of these refugees and their experiences: Why did they leave Vietnam? How did they leave? What other alternatives might they have had? How did they like the conditions at Camp Pendleton? What kind of employment prospects were they looking forward to?

Perhaps the most dramatic feature of the Vietnamese situation was the total lack of accurate information about the military defeat in Saigon before the evacuation began. Available information indicates that the American government had plans to evacuate refugees at least three weeks before the event took place. Had the military and government authorities prepared the people of Vietnam for such plans, three weeks would have given adequate time for an orderly exodus for those desiring to leave Vietnam.

Yet, preparation was nonexistent. The majority of the refugees had no time to prepare. (See Table 1.) More than half indicated they had less than ten hours to evacuate, 61 percent indicated having less than twenty-four hours and 83 percent indicated a time span less than one week. In such a short time, it is not easy to decide whether to leave or stay. One refugee reported: "Mother came along to the airport. Then at the last minute, she stayed behind because the number of children staying was larger than those leaving."

Table 1

AMOUNT OF TIME TO EVACUATE

Time	Frequency	Percentage	Cumulative Percentage
Less than an hour	17	28.8	28.8
1 to 10 hours	15	25.4	54.2
10 to 24 hours	4	6.8	61.0
24 to 48 hours	2	3.4	64.4
3 to 7 days	11	18.6	83.1
1 to 2 weeks	4	6.8	89.8
2 to 4 weeks	2	3.4	93.2
More than 4 weeks	2	3.4	96.6
Other	2	3.4	100.0

Apparently, the military and political situation in Vietnam deteriorated so rapidly, the refugees were caught off guard. (While there is no methodological justification for generalizing the Camp

Pendleton data to refugees in other camps, there is no reason either to believe it atypical.) Consider when the refugees left Vietnam. (See Table 2.)

The departure from Vietnam was accomplished mostly in the week of April 25-May 1, 1975. Prior to April 25, 1975, only 3 percent of the refugees had departed, and after May 1 another 3.4 percent departed. Between April 25 and April 30, 93 percent of the sample left Vietnam. In two days, April 29 and 30, 75 percent of our sample left Vietnam. This is a very short span of time for mass evacuation.

Table 2

DATE OF VIETNAM DEPARTURE

Date	Frequency	Percentage	Cumulative Percentage
Before April 25	2	3.4	3.4
Between April 25 and 28	11	18.6	22.0
On April 29	18	30.5	52.5
On April 30	26	44.1	96.6
First week in May	2	3.4	100.0
Total	59	100.0	100.0

Literally within a few hours, thousands of Vietnamese with their entire or partial families had become refugees with no employment and few meaningful symbols to identify their status. The sudden change of status and identity was not accompanied by sufficient time to prepare them for the instant "refugee status" they had to assume quickly. They became part of the statistics typical of violent political and military transactions.

Table 3 indicates the three major reasons given by heads of households for leaving Vietnam. Fifty-seven percent were alarmed by the bad military and political news, twenty-six percent were afraid of reprisals by the Communists, and ten percent felt they could not live under the communist regime. Seven percent of this sample did not make a rational decision to flee but somehow were caught up in the evacuation and just went along. The decision-making process then varied from those who made a rational decision that flight was necessary in view of their own past activities or job positions, to those whose lack of information precluded their knowing they had made a decision.

Table 3

FIRST THING THAT MADE YOU THINK YOU MUST LEAVE VIETNAM

	Frequency	Percentage
Afraid of reprisals	16	26.2
Situation in Vietnam	35	54.4
Just went along	4	6.6
Communists closing in	6	9.8
		100.00

According to 57 percent of the sample, the situation in Vietnam had deteriorated so much by the end of April, they had to leave their homeland. News came of the rapid downfall of many provinces—Nha Trad, Bien Hoa, Vung Tau, Phan Thiet, Ban Methuot, Khanh Dvong, Danang, and Long Khah. This bad news made the Vietnamese think that the fall of Vietnam was imminent. There was "loss of lots of territory to the Communists." One Vietnamese stated, "There was a province lost each day." An experienced serviceman stated, "in the past, it took many days to take over a province. Many provinces fell within one day, so the fall of Vietnam was imminent."

Rapid falls of cities were related by former soldier-refugees: "The commanding officers had abandoned their posts. The base was deserted due to the evacuations. The enemy was just about to attack our base, and I thought we just did not have enough forces to resist."

Others who guessed Vietnam would fall to the Communists in the near future gave the following individual assessments of the military situation prior to their evacuation: "Communist takeover of (Army Regions) I and II Corps made me think that the country will fall imminently, so I must leave Vietnam." "The Second Army Region was lost while the U.S. Congress was still debating." "Vietnam was bound to go Communist because the army was very weak and afraid of reprisal; we had to go away against our will."

The Communists took over the areas around Saigon. There was fear that "fighting would soon come to my province, so we left to avoid shelling and firing." Another person stated, "The Communists were advancing to Saigon—too close to my house." Saigon was being shelled on the 28th and 29th of April. North Vietnamese aircraft were attacking. This shelling was the reason for the evacuation of one respondent who stated: "Saw too much fighting, too frightened, had to run away from the shelling but did not have any plan about going away for good." Dissolution of ARVN on April 29, 1975, also was given as a reason for evacuation.

News of Big Minh concerned the Vietnamese, especially the surrender. "Since the NLF forced General Minh to become President, then to surrender, thought then it was time to run away." Another respondent said he "knew right away we must leave Vietnam when he heard from Radio Saigon about the turnover of government to Big Minh."

United States actions prompted seven respondents to evacuate. According to one Vietnamese man, "The U.S. setback in the Middle East led to scarcity in oil, which in turn shot up everything, which in turn led to reassessment of U.S. policy in Indochina. The loss of Cambodia is a lesson of reality which will happen to Vietnam. This is a strain to all educated Vietnamese people." Another Vietnamese told the interviewer, "The U.S. embassy and other embassies closed, the three U.S. banks closed and flew their personnel out. These three actions showed me the emergency of the situation and eventually the imminent downfall of Vietnam." Evacuation of all U.S. personnel caused concern. The time to evacuate was short, even for the U.S. personnel. "After the shutdown of the TSN airport on April 29th, the news was that all U.S. personnel must be out of Vietnam within twenty-four hours."

One man who worked for a U.S. company said he "saw U.S. personnel preparing to leave. They let Vietnamese personnel come along, so I knew eventually Vietnam will fall to the Communists." One household head stated, "Just about everybody around us packed up and was ready for take off." The evacuation panic and disorder was blamed by one eyewitness on the U.S. because "funds were cut off by the U.S. and the news of U.S. betrayal of their Vietnamese allies circulated."

The 26 percent who were afraid of reprisals were mostly military personnel, government civil servants, and Catholics. Examples of the statements they made to the interviewer are:

"Thought the Communists would never accept a former ARVN officer." "Being in the Vietnamese navy, my life was in danger of reprisal." "Because I was in the ARVN—threat to my life during the changeover." "Afraid of reprisal by enemy upon the military rank and file." "Being an educated, high-ranking officer attached to the police state, I was afraid I would die by Communists' hands." "My husband is a high ranking civil servant, trained in the U.S., and working with the Americans in Vietnam. We were afraid of reprisal and death."

Catholics, as a group, felt they would be singled out and subjected to reprisals. One interviewee stated, "Catholics have co-existed with the Communists before and we know we would not be spared." The general feeling was that the Catholics would be unable to remain in Vietnam. "People in my parish say the Catholics would not have a chance to survive under the Communists. And, on top of that, we are from the North fleeing southward in 1954." Many escape attempts were desperate. In some cases, refugees were caught up in the force of events and originally had no intention of leaving the country. They either made an on-the-spot determination to do so or were physically unable to remove themselves from the exiting stream.

One middle-aged woman who worked for an American-operated broadcasting company accidentally overheard the news about the collapse of the Saigon military defense in the middle of April. When she confronted her boss with what she heard over the British Broadcasting Company, he abruptly denied the news was true. A few days later she went to the pharmacy to purchase medicine and was told the supply was exhausted and a new shipment was not expected. The woman then came to the conclusion that the defense of Saigon was doomed to fail.

The lack of planning, preparation, and resources is strikingly evident in most cases. A large number of Vietnamese followed the crowd, unaware of where they were going. They had no idea they were leaving the country. People said: "I saw everyone running to the harbor, so I decide to go along." "Friends wanted me to come along for fun; I did not know it was an evacuation." When they reached the Philippines, one family found out they were bound for the United States. Their response: "We did not plan on taking this trip." These people were caught in unsafe military situations, amidst panic and fear, and were caught in the rush of people evacuating.

Military personnel followed their superiors. One respondent said he had no intention of leaving Vietnam, but, as a serviceman, he had to obey his superior officer. Military orders were given for him to follow his superior on board ship, and he had no idea where the ship was going. There was apparently no adequate information about the military situation of the war. Many had become so accustomed to depending upon the Americans for direction, they panicked when they saw Americans evacuating Vietnam. Neither the American government nor the Vietnamese government had made adequate plans to give clear instruction and information to the people. Perhaps the government was uncertain what would happen. A total collapse of the normal social and normative structures resulted before adequate preparation for the actual evacuation took place. The result was a series of human tragedies.

Refugees were interviewed only a few days after their arrival at Camp Pendleton. In order to capture their vivid experience, their anxieties, hopes, and frustrations, one question asked for a detailed account of their escape experience. Much of the accounts related to their sudden awareness of the necessity to leave Vietnam. Some related to events *en route* to the United States. When asked about their most dramatic events, an amazingly high proportion of the refugees could not say anything. The "blanking out" of their traumatic experience of flight and anxieties may not be surprising considering the circumstances. However, more than half (54.3 percent) did give some account of "dramatic events," most related to their flight experience involving loss of life-long savings, being cut off from relatives, or the witnessing of the fall of the city. Many did mention personal experience of being bombed and shelled by enemy fire. Some described scenes which caused mass panic. Table 4 summarizes themes mentioned by refugees.

About half of the Vietnamese stated they felt panic, fear, concern, and worry during the week prior to evacuation. Suspense and threat filled their lives. Many stated the above fears in a generalized way without giving specific events. One Vietnamese gave this description: "Witnessed people around me worried without daring to show their concern. This was also true for my family. We were very much in a state of suspense and fear up to a point of not being able to eat or sleep. News and rumors converging from all places render nerves so tense."

Table 4

MOST DRAMATIC EVENT DURING THE LAST WEEK IN VIETNAM

	Frequency	Percentage
Worried, frightened	18	48.7
Loss of fortune	3	8.1
Loss of relatives	6	16.2
Fall of Vietnam	1	2.7
Bombing, Shelling	4	10.8
Panic Scenes	4	10.8
No news	1	2.7
Total	37	100.0%

Fear of the Communists was stated in this way: "I was concerned because the Communists advanced so close to our home." "We worried about what will happen to us in case of a Communist takeover. We still do not have any news of the fate of our relatives who stayed behind." Fear of reprisals and deaths when the Communists arrived was stated by one Vietnamese in this way, "I was panicked, afraid of the killings when the Communists came to town."

Other Vietnamese reported feeling fearful and panicky because of the Communist shellings. One person stated, "My entire family was panicked and frightened because of the shelling and attack right at the outskirts of Saigon." Another Vietnamese "met many refugees coming into town and was fearful because the town was under shelling." One Vietnamese stated, "I was afraid they would shell right into my home," and another reported seeing "an entire family wounded and one child killed." During the last week in Vietnam, many were worried about escaping. One worried whether or not they would be able to escape. Another Vietnamese stated his worry in this way, "I was in a state of fear and panic during the whole week—searching for a way to escape. All my brothers and sisters were together during that period until the end when a solution was found. Then, we got lost and must be separated forever." Just how desperate the Vietnamese were can be felt by this person's statement, "All other events aside, I only worried about getting out of Vietnam. My children in Germany called long-distance and told me to leave the country by any means."

It appears that the plans for evacuation could not be discussed openly. According to one refugee, "Everybody was worried and frightened and talked in secret about leaving." The Vietnamese were unable to discuss leaving even with some relatives. Fear prevailed and was stated in this way, "Concern and worry was all around us. Our relatives and monks from the nearby pagoda looked suspicious and might be undercover Viet Cong agents or others opposed to the Thieu regime." The Vietnamese evacuation events were unlike the events leading to the evacuation of Japanese Americans in California during World War II. They got in touch with their relatives.

Loss of family members was stated by 16.2 percent of our sample as the most dramatic event during the last week of evacuation. These family separations caused much heartbreak. One man left behind all his relatives and loved ones: his mother, two sons, brother, mother-in-law, and uncles. Another former Vietnamese soldier left behind his aged mother, son, and two daughters, knowing they could never be reunited. One man told the interviewer he "had to accept his wife's decision to remain behind with her family." Individuals indicated concern about relatives and family members living in the Viet Cong area.

Loss of fortune was indicated by 8.1 percent of the Vietnamese as the most dramatic event during the last week of evacuation. Leaving behind all one's belongings is sad. One interviewee stated, "I regretted having to leave all the labor of a lifetime behind, and also my family."

News was important to the Vietnamese during the final week before they left Vietnam. Some had no access to news as these two statements show, "No news. Did not know what was going on." "Isolated from the rest of the coutry. Was in Vung Tau which was cut off from everything." One person told the interviewer of "running all over place looking for acquaintances to find out what was going on." Others told how they waited for "news from outside."

The first step taken by the Vietnamese to make departing possible was varied. (See Table 5.) The largest number, nine heads of households, had no plans before they left Vietnam. Some who boarded ships without any difficulty made the following statements: "Took no steps. Only boarded ship to go and eventually ended up here in the United States." "No steps. Only saw Vietnamese navy ship picking up the people, so I jumped in." "No steps taken. Ship moored by the harbor and anyone was free to come aboard." "Did not take any steps at all. Left too suddenly. Went from police headquarters in Saigon to harbor closeby and boarded ship with no trouble at all." "No steps. Only saw that the Vietnamese navy allowed transportation means, so I took my family aboard."

Table **5**

STEPS TAKEN TO LEAVE

A)   First Step Taken to Make Departing Vietnam Possible

Step	Frequency	Percentage
Got Proper Papers	6	10.2
Worked for American	3	5.1
Got onto Viet Ship	6	10.2
Help from Friends	8	13.6
Went in Fishing Junk	5	8.5
Knew Nothing	1	1.7
No Difficulty	1	1.7
No Plans Beforehand	9	15.3
All Taken Care of	2	3.4
Others	14	23.7
No response	4	6.8
Total	59	100.0

B)   Second Step Taken

Step	Frequency	Percentage
Got Proper Papers	1	1.7
Worked for American	1	1.7
Got onto Viet Ship	5	8.5
Help from Friends	1	1.7
Went in Fishing Junk	2	3.4
No Difficulty	1	1.7
No Plans Beforehand	1	1.7
Others	7	5.1
Skip	40	67.8
Total	59	100.0

"Watched many people leaving from Saigon Harbor on April 29. On April 30, took the whole family out to the harbor, asked to go along, and were let aboard ship for the trip." Others who did not take any steps for leaving Vietnam had other family members take care of everything, for example this woman: "I did nothing . . . daughter-in-law took care of all the formalities."

Thirteen percent of those interviewed said they received assistance from friends and relatives. Connections were important. Those who were in the navy or knew someone in the navy had a vehicle by which to leave Vietnam. Answers of this kind are: "Was in Vietnamese navy so had a place aboard ship." "Help from a nephew, a navy officer, who guided us to the naval base to get aboard ship." "No need to have papers. Have a brother in the navy who took us along to the navy headquarters and we boarded ship for the trip." "Cousin was a navy commander, took us aboard ship at McCarthy Pier at Cam Ranh Bay. We went out to sea, went with the Vietnamese Navy to Phu Quoc Island, to Singapore, to Subic Bay, to Guam and to the U.S.A."

Getting the proper papers to leave was the first step in the process for six Vietnamese families. Two individuals submitted papers proving they worked for U.S. agencies. Often relatives and friends were able to help secure the proper papers for leaving. Following are four such examples showing the importance of connections:

"Had all papers with me—daughter got the paper for me, took me to the TSN airport, got inside with help from brother who was a security agent for MACV, then got processed out."

"My brother-in-law, an ICSS coordinator, took care of all the processing of papers."

"Brother, a colonel in ARVN took care of all paper work for the whole family to leave Vietnam."

"A Vietnamese friend obtained an affidavit of support for me from the U.S. embassy. Showed the ID card and affidavit at the TSN airport."

If a person's name was on the U.S. embassy's evacuation list, departure was facilitated.

To depart from Vietnam, 22 percent of the sample sought an evacuation vehicle. There were six Vietnamese heads of households who tried to board a ship, five who departed by junks, and two who left by plane. One head of household "bribed way into naval shipyard" to board a ship, and another reported that they "silently found way to the harbor and bribed way aboard ship."

One family "went along with friends looking for a ship to go to Singapore." Another Vietnamese "asked the Philippines consular services to board Philippine vessel departing from Vietnam."

If a fishing junk was owned by the family or relatives, escape was easier. An example of this kind of response: "Had a relative's boat ready. Only had to stock it with food and fuel. Nothing else to worry about." Finding a junk was sometimes difficult. One head of household in this predicament stated "I worked on my own, went from Saigon to Van Tau and then found and rented a junk to go offshore to the U.S. ship." Another Vietnamese "discussed with friends how to get aboard ship and drifted offshore for the entire week."

Statements from Vietnamese who departed by plane:

"Friends of husband came and took us to the airbase to wait for the departing plane." "Tried to find out which is the evacuation plane, tried to get onto it and go to Con Son Island where all our relatives were." "Boarded evacuation plane by showing proper identification which indicated my two sons are U.S. citizens."

Vietnamese who worked for American companies had no problems with transportation. Some examples of responses given by people with job-related access to vehicles:

"Worked for a shipping firm so had means of transportation." "Was allowed to be evacuated because I worked for U.S. company. Put name on evacuation list, but it was too late for that on the last day. Was picked up by a helicopter." "Went along with company, radio station VOA-VOF-AA, therefore did not need any papers." "Husband worked for the U.S. DAO so we went to the Philippines."

The Vietnamese prepared to leave Vietnam. One stated they "stocked up necessary items such as fuel, oil, and food two weeks before departure date." Another stated his desperation and fear in this way: "Packed up a few daily-used clothes and biographic papers. Waited until the last minute. If the Communists should take over Saigon, then we will have to flee. Am ready to pay any price, suffer any hardship, even at the risk of death." Two Vietnamese who tried to get away from the firing zone made these statements, "Took the family to a safer area, away from the firing zone." "Tried to find means to get to the harbor and to leave Vietnam. When we boarded ship we left everything behind under bombing." This bombing caused some families to try to leave more permanently as described by this Vietnamese: "When (Region) I and II Army corps fell, we went out to sea, intermittently we came back to old home. Arrived in Vung Tau but were under fire, so decided to leave for good and go to Hong Kong. Offshore met U.S. ship, boarded, and came to the United States."

Asked to describe the kinds of problems encountered in the attempt to leave Vietnam, 37 percent responded "none." The other thirty eight household heads described forty problems. (See Table 6.)

Table **6**

PROBLEMS ENCOUNTERED IN ATTEMPT TO LEAVE VIETNAM

Problem	Frequency	Percentage
Get onto Ship, Plane	10	25
Get into Evacuation Area	12	30
Lack Evacuation Vehicle	2	5
Secure Evacuation Papers	2	5
Lack Fuel	2	5
Lack Food	3	7.5
Others	9	22.5
Total	40	100.0

The military situation, the lack of adequate and decisive action, and the confusion created by the lack of authoritative information were all responsible for the lack of means and goals of evacuation. "What to do?" was the question. One was not sure just what to do, who to follow, or even with whom to talk because of the maximum amount of ambiguity. At this time it is understandable that many refugees had fear as to the specific course of action in order to escape. More than 50 percent of the Vietnamese reported having difficulty reaching a safe place or finding the means to escape to a safe place, when in fact none knew just where a safe place was.

The Vietnamese reported having problems getting into the evacuation area. One stated they "had to fight to get into the plant to board the helicopter." Other responses expressed this kind of problem and these solutions: "Not allowed to get into the evacuation area, but we followed higher ranking superiors." "I bribed the guards because passing the gate of the naval shipyard was so difficult." "Had a problem entering the airbase but was helped by husband's friends who work inside the base." "Cannot get into navy headquarters, so I looked for nephew who was a navy officer."

Another common problem was how to board the evacuation vehicle. Vietnamese went out to sea in the hopes of being picked up by the U.S. ships. One head of household stated "how to get to sea" was his biggest problem until he found a commercial boat which belonged to other escapees. Once at sea, concerns then centered on whether they would be picked up. This concern is described: "No other problems besides that of getting out to sea to get picked up by U.S. ships. We did not know whether we would meet the U.S. ships or not." "From Saigon, went to sea, but U.S. ship declined to pick us up. We just had to keep on drifting even when we ran out of provisions." A Vietnamese navy skipper, who was in charge of the base, came to the rescue of one family who was looking for a ship to escape from Phu Quoc. Another Vietnamese stated, "Navy authorities did not allow us to board ship. The problem was solved when the Vietnamese navy was routed (dissolved) so there were no more complications with anyone."

After the military was defeated, the primary concern of the Vietnamese turned from fighting the enemy to saving their own lives. All their energy was devoted to overcoming the obstacles between them and a place of safety. Under these circumstances, it is not surprising to see defeated soldiers threatening the lives of civilians perceived as threats to their safety instead of defending them. Such problems with the Vietnamese military was the concern of two Vietnamese heads of households. One reported, "Vietnamese soldiers wanted to take over the junk. I ran away, was very lucky." The other reported, "ARVN boarded our ship and forced us to take them to different places. I solved this problem by using low-key convincing words to assure them all will be well."

Securing an evacuation vehicle was difficult for two Vietnamese families. One head of household stated, "Borrowed a GMC truck to get from Dalat and Cam Ranh Bay, which was crowded with Vietnamese marines and soldiers. Borrowed an LCP to get to bigger ship offshore." Another head of household stated he had "no car to take the family to the harbor." He used a motorbike and took many trips back and forth.

This last heroic effort indicates the effort made by many Vietnamese to escape in family groups, to bring out their whole (extended) families.

Other problems described included securing valid papers, lack of financial means to leave the country, lack of food supplies, no agencies or organizations to get help in leaving Vietnam, and boat problems including no steering, no crank-shaft, and no fuel.

Characteristic solutions of refugees.—The details and particulars of the Vietnamese refugees' flight defy summation but give vividness to their highly individualistic solutions so different from the voluntary immigrant. Louise Holborn has argued that there is a distinction between the "refugee" and the "immigrant," but the "refugee" status is transitory. Once the refugee leaves the economic and political uncertainties of the "midway to nowhere," he ceases to be a refugee, and his attitudes and behavior are the same as a voluntary immigrant.

Holborn's thesis has two major difficulties: First, on the research level, there is a lack of conceptual distinction between the refugee and the voluntary migrant with respect to the conditions under which movement took place and under what motivation. The latter may particularly confuse the research issue. Many contemporary researchers tend to raise questions about refugee adjustment in the United States in the same way they research questions about immigrants. This may give erroneous conclusions and interpretations of the research data. Second, on the level of services and programs designed to assist refugee adjustment, to treat refugees as immigrants means there are no more official responsibilities to be discharged. Those who treat refugees as immigrants are apt to be more interested in the political or military event which created the refugees than the problems of the refugees themselves:

"The refugee must be distinguished conceptually from the voluntary migrant, since, with a different past and with motivations at variance with those affecting voluntary migrants, the refugee moves from his homeland to the country of his settlement against his will. He is a distinct social type. He is, according to the internationally accepted definition, an individual who owing to well-founded fear of being persecuted for reasons of race, reli-

gion, nationality, membership in a particular social group of political opinion, is outside the country of his nationality and is unable, or owing to such fear, unwilling to avail himself of the protection of that country; or, who, not having a nationality or being outside the country of his former habitual residence as a result of such events, is unable or, owing to such fear, is unwilling to return to it. It is the reluctance to uproot oneself, and the absence of positive original motivations to settle elsewhere, which characterizes all refugee decisions and distinguishes the refugee from the voluntary migrants."—Kunz, 1973, p. 130

Kunz's distinction seems to have important implications for the ultimate adjustment of the refugee inasmuch as the refugee and voluntary migrant have different frames of reference. To employ here Rotter's concept of locus of control (Rotter, 1966), the *voluntary migrant* has made a fairly rational decision, based on elements of planning, estimated rewards and costs, and anticipated status improvements, etc.—all under control of the migrant. The refugee often has no real decision to make, no control over means and destination, few resources, and unless aided by the government looks forward to uncontrolled deterioration rather than improvement in his life circumstances.

Kunz employs what he calls a kinetic model, analogous to a billiard ball, in which the refugee goes from one geographic location to another in response to the forces of others; if he meets no resistance, he goes in the direction he is sent by events; if he does, he goes another direction. He may find himself in circumstances providing few opportunities, in which he is barely welcome. The situation may be unsuited to his particular linguistic and vocational competence and may separate him from important significant others such as family. Most important here is his psychological readiness to take advantage of whatever opportunities exist and to adjust to circumstances. The refugee is not motivated to make this change in his life. He is without goals, he has the feeling of having lost control of his life and destiny. He is in an essentially involuntary relationship (Thibaut and Kelley, 1959) with few or no alternatives. This is when psychiatric symptoms such as depression flourish. Depression, almost by definition, is the outcome of continuing in an undesirable situation which cannot be altered.

Typology of refugee flight—"Acute" flight patterns of the

Vietnamese.—Kunz differentiates refugee movements into subtypes. First, the *anticipatory refugee movement.* The refugee leaves his home country in an orderly and well-prepared way before complete deterioration, and there is some superficial resemblance to voluntary migration, although it is the push rather than the pull which is compelling. The other type is the *acute.* There are also situations called *intermediate* which lie between the acute and the anticipatory:

"Acute refugee movements contrast with anticipatory movements sharply both in their selectiveness and their kinetics. Acute refugee movements arise from great political changes or movements of armies. The refugees flee either in mass flight or, if their flight is obstructed, in bursts of individual or group escapes, and their primary purpose is to reach safety in a neighboring or nearby country which will grant them asylum. The emphasis is on the escape and, at the time of passing through the border, few refugees partaking in acute movements are aware that later further migration will become a necessity."—Kunz, 1973, p. 132

The refugee status has an anomalous and ambiguous character. Although there is often resistance to its termination, it is never envisioned as anything but a temporary status. Refugee status derives its meaning from the events precipitating it. It is meaningful only as the end product of political and military events and the situation of the refugee in these events. It does not have the future orientation of the voluntary migrant status—the individual utopia of improved social, material, and religious circumstances. This provides a goal and gives meaning to the struggle to adjust to uncomfortable and unfamiliar surroundings. There is pressure to move on physically and psychologically from temporary asylum, from where the refugee fantasizes a victorious return to the homeland but gradually comes to a realization:

"In the course of the exciting and dramatic events, he miscalculated and there will be no victorious return. At this stage the refugee still does not look forward but already knows that the door's bar closed behind him. . . . Subsequent administrative, economic, and psychological pressures may force him to make a further step and to become an immigrant in a country willing to receive him. This pressure following the original push, whether it eventuates in the form of the freezing of charity funds, the forcing

of refugees into uncongenial refugee camps, the offer of assisted passages or other actions intended to move him, appears to be always more decisive than the pull of the country where the refugee eventually goes."—Kunz, 1973: 133

In other words, exit from refugee status is in some ways as involuntary as entry. The refugee resists termination of direct assistance and reclassification as a voluntary immigrant.

The survey of fifty-nine heads of households carried out at Camp Pendleton, if applicable to all refugees, suggests that the recent exodus from Vietnam was principally of the "acute" flight pattern. As noted before, 85 percent had just a few days or less and 54 percent no more than ten hours to prepare to leave. To put it in another way, fifty-six out of fifty-nine families of refugee households for which we have detailed interview records fled during the last week in April, forty-four on the last two days.

Kunz points out:

"Both anticipatory and acute refugee movements may become a social force, carrying with them individuals who have neither much to fear nor much to lose. Even if the underlying causes of such departures are an inflated view of the individual's importance, incorrect judgments, or his succumbing to the epidemics of fear and hope, the person who takes flight under the pressures of the social force of pervasive flight-attitudes must be considered still a refugee. The validity of fear for one's safety which is the creator of all refugees can after all never be tested: it is the individual's interpretation of events and self-perceived danger or revulsion, or role, which motivates the refugee and justifies his stand."—Kunz, 1973:136

One of the crucial factors in the evacuation was the lack of adequate information about the current military and political situation in Saigon. This produced at least believable rumors about a blood-bath that would occur when Communist soldiers marched into the city. Once the fear was heightened, it was not difficult to fall in with any course of action, so long as such actions might lead to safety.

Fourteen of the fifty-nine, or almost 25 percent, did not discuss evacuation with anyone, in some cases, because they did not intend to evacuate. The list of persons consulted first by the household heads regarding departure from Vietnam is quite varied, as shown in Table 7. Twenty-two percent of the household heads first talked things over with their spouses. Ten percent talked about leaving their homeland with brothers. Another 19 percent first talked with different family members: their own parents, spouse's parents, grandparents, uncles, and cousins. Non-relatives were consulted by 17 percent of the household heads. Finally, 17 percent made the decision to leave by themselves without talking to anyone.

Table 7

FIRST PERSON WITH WHOM HOUSEHOLD HEADS TALKED ABOUT LEAVING VIETNAM

Relationship to Household Head	Frequency	Percentage
Spouse	13	22.2
Father	1	1.7
Mother	2	3.4
Spouse's Father	2	3.4
Brother	6	10.2
Spouse's Brother	1	1.7
Grandfather	1	1.7
Uncle	2	3.4
Cousin	2	3.4
Non-Relative	10	16.9
Nobody	10	16.9
Others	4	6.8
No response	5	8.5
Total	59	100.0

Fifty-nine heads of households gave 107 reasons for why they felt it was important to leave Vietnam. (See Table 8.) One group had left North Vietnam in 1954 because of their anti-Communist sentiments and fear of reprisals.

Previous to 1954, 59 percent of the heads of households lived in North Vietnam (north of the 17th Parallel) and 41 percent lived in South Vietnam. These people were not strangers to fleeing. An experienced refugee stated, "I do not accept Communist life because my family already gave up everything fleeing in 1954 for freedom. We work for the government and ARVN and are afraid of reprisal." Three other Vietnamese statements of reasons for fleeing: (1) "Because I worked in the French Colonial Army, I was afraid of being eliminated so I fled from North to South in 1954." (2) "I lived with the Communist (underground) prior to

1954; I fled then and am now fearful of reprisal." (3) "I cannot live under the Communist regime because already I experienced such a life in 1954 during the exchange of prisoners between the Communist and French forces."

Table **8**

MOST IMPORTANT REASONS GIVEN FOR LEAVING VIETNAM

Reason	Frequency	Percentage
Anti-Communism	38	35.5
Afraid of Reprisals	24	22.4
1954 Refugee from North Vietnam	10	9.3
In the Military	9	8.4
Past Experiences	5	4.6
Worked for Americans	5	4.6
Future for Children	5	4.6
Being a Catholic	4	3.7
Just Went Along	2	1.8
Other Reasons	2	1.8
No Response	3	3.7

Some Vietnamese were carefully prepared with papers but did not know exactly when to leave and had some difficulties. Others discussed and rationally devised *ad hoc* plans, making use of papers or contacts. In answer to "Did you have any other plans or ideas about what you and your family could do instead of leaving Vietnam?" fifty-four heads of households, 75 percent, replied "no alternatives." They had run out of options. When asked: "Did you have alternatives if you did not leave Vietnam as you did?" Typical answers were: "Do anything to get out of Vietnam." "No other solution but to escape Vietnam." "No alternative—totally dependent on the situation in Vietnam if have to stay behind." "Ran away with the panicking crowd." "Did not know I was leaving Vietnam but boarded ship with the thought only of running away from the shelling." (See Table 9.)

Anti-Communism was stated by thirty-eight out of fifty-nine respondents. Ten heads of households stated they could not accept the Communist regime or could not co-exist with the Communists. Five household heads stated they could not stand living under a Communist regime and wanted to avoid Communists. Others indicated a fear of the Communists. One expressed his fear in this way, "I seek freedom. Am afraid I will be miserable of Communists and of strange new regime."

Table 9

DID YOU HAVE ALTERNATIVES IF YOU DID NOT LEAVE VIETNAM?

	Frequency	Percentage
Yes	13	22.0
No	43	72.9
No Answer	3	5.1
	59	100.0

At least eight of the families indicated having previous experiences living with the Communists. Statements given in regard to their unwillingness to live again with the Communists: (1) "Do not want to live with Communists because my mother experienced it." (2) "My father experienced life with the Communists and you cannot live with them." (3) "Threat of my own life through past experiences." Bad past experiences existed for the Vietnamese when they attempted to live with the Communists. An experience shared by a 1954 refugee was, "My father was killed because he worked for the French. Our home was destroyed. We had to move for the future of my children."

Twenty-four of the fifty-nine heads of households indicated fear of Communist reprisals as an important reason for leaving Vietnam. Their previous employment as military personnel, government employees, and U.S. agency workers placed them in this difficult position. Following are examples of statements made to the interviewers:

"Afraid of reprisal because husband interrogated Communist prisoners for U.S. forces in Vietnam." "Afraid of reprisal because my wife and I worked with U.S. agency for more than thirteen years." "Afraid of treatment reserved by Communists for former Vietnamese navy men." "Afraid of death under the Communists because I was a serviceman in the Navy." "Afraid of the Communists because I am a serviceman. I do not think the Communists would forgive my family and myself." "Was in the intelligence division in the police force. I thought it would be impossible to stay behind in Vietnam." "Fear of execution for two reasons: (1) Fled from North Vietnam in 1954. (2) Work in the police force for the anti-Communist propaganda division."

Worry and fear for their children's future was given by five respondents as the reason for departing from Vietnam. Concern for their children's future was stated by the Vietnamese in this way: "I seek freedom so my children can carry on their education until graduation." "I am afraid if my children had to live under the Communist regime."

Other reasons for leaving Vietnam: (1) the belief Catholics would not be accepted, (2) to get away from the fighting and shelling, (3) married to an American with two Asian-American children. Two Vietnamese indicated they had no intention of coming to the United States. They did not want to leave their homeland.

Three heads of households considered suicide as an alternative to leaving Vietnam. One made this statement: "First, disperse family members to different places. As for myself will either commit suicide or let the Communists finish me." Others considered "returning to the countryside so that no one will recognize us. Avoid everything for a while to see what will happen." "Stay in Vietnam and do farming." "Go into hiding in Vietnam and find a way to escape later on—anywhere." "Will go into hiding; wait and see as things develop. Cannot coexist with the Communists. If only they behave as any other people, we would be willing to live with them. Besides, I was in the service and there could be misjudgment during the change of regime which could lead to reprisal and killing. That is why my family and myself had to flee." The other alternative considered was continued fighting as stated by these two Vietnamese: "Join the Hao Hao sect into the jungle and carry on fighting." "Go into guerrilla warfare."

The refugees were not immigrants who chose to come to America for the opportunities. Rather, they left Vietnam because they felt they had no choice. Their migration was not a matter of premeditated adventure. They were extremely desperate, with very little time to salvage their lives from the impending danger.

Many refugees were confused as to where they were when received at the camp, then were surprised when told they were in California. A large number of the refugees could not believe they were in the United States at the time of the interview. They were not allowed out of the camp site and were surrounded by barren hills. Visitors and interviewers frequently were asked if indeed they were in the United States. Communication with the outside world was set up poorly in the beginning. There were only a few pay phone booths for the entire camp. They were set up at the administrative office areas with long queues of people trying to reach their friends or relatives outside. Few of the refugees had thought of escaping to the United States when the exodus took place. Perhaps this was why many were surprised when told the Marine camp was located in California. In order to substantiate some of the observers' impressions, refugees were asked: "Which country was your first choice as a final destination when you left Vietnam?" About one-half finally admitted that America would be their first choice with some initial hesitations. Such answers could not be accepted at face value since the refugees knew at the time they were in America, in an American military camp. Consistent with other information was the fact that the second largest category of response was that no country was their first choice inasmuch as they really did not think about leaving Vietnam. This is shown in Table 10.

Table 10

WHICH COUNTRY WAS FIRST CHOICE?

	Frequency	Percentage
U.S.A.	26	49.1
France	6	11.3
Australia	2	3.8
Germany	1	1.9
Thailand	1	1.9
Philippines	1	1.9
None	12	22.6
Others	2	3.8
Don't Know	2	3.8

For whatever reason, about one-half of the heads of households stated that America was their first choice. The reason given by one woman for choosing the United States was, "because we only know English, and my husband likes the Americans. We had opportunities to work with them and liked them."

Twelve heads of households did not indicate any country as

their first choice. Approximately one third, even at this point, did not have a specific country of refuge in mind, indicating once again the lack of positive pull factors for their movement. Typical reasons given for this lack of choice were: "Did not think of any country. Only wanted to go offshore to avoid shelling." "Did not plan on going anywhere. Only took family offshore to run away from shelling, waited till it was over to go back to go ashore; however, I met U.S. ship which picked us up and brought us here." "No country. Did not think of any nation even when aboard evacuation ship."

France was chosen by 11.3 percent of the respondents as their first choice for evacuation. Some of this sample had relatives in France. One opinion of living in France was, "We have relatives in France, brother, sister, and mother. French people do not mistreat the Vietnamese, are kind and life is easier to cope with there. Food is also easier to adjust to." Reasons for not going to France were: "France did not accept any refugees due to unemployment." "French government requires husbands to go to France first to secure employment before family can go over." "No means. Ship went to Singapore, then directly to the United States." "Political situation in France was not suitable."

Other countries considered by the Vietnamese were Australia, Germany, Thailand, and the Philippines. In any case, countries of the first choice coincided with the lack of alternative plans. Refugees made decisions of circumstances or, more simply, decisions of no alternatives. The following excerpts were illuminating:

"Afraid not to be accepted and welcomed so fled to the United States." "We have a son in Germany, and we were waiting for visa to go to Germany." "Australia did not accept refugees then." "It was too far for the boat, which was out of order, to reach Australia. That place lacks too many daily life conveniences." "Planned to go to Australia, but changed mind in Singapore because thought that in the U.S. can get more help and more opportunities." "On the way to Hong Kong, met U.S. ship bound for the U.S., so boarded and came here." "Headed for Thailand. Picked up by U.S. ship and sent directly to the U.S." "More likely to get adjusted better in the States with all the help provided by the U.S. government." "Nearest land by boat. Singapore was our destination. If not accepted by the Singapore government, go to the nearest place by land."

In spite of nearly half of the respondents saying that America was their first choice, most were thinking about other places in the beginning. Detailed interviews revealed that many refugees did not expect to go to the United States. Many thought of locating in Thailand, Singapore, or Hong Kong. America was thought to be too far from Vietnam and therefore was not included in their possibilities as a safe haven. Thus, many refugees later told the interviewers they were surprised when they found themselves in California. Many could not even believe it. Perhaps America was an ideal place to go, but certainly it was not planned that way.

One would expect with such lack of preparation and often lack of planning and decision that regrets might exist. Yet, to the question, "Do you regret leaving Vietnam?" the majority or 54.2 percent responded *no* and 11.9 percent responded *uncertain.* (See Table 11.) The 33.9 percent who responded *yes* gave forty-four reasons why they were sorry they left Vietnam. Most often given reasons were loss of relatives, loss of homeland, and loss of fortune. (See Table 12.)

Table 11

DO YOU REGRET LEAVING VIETNAM?

	Frequency	Percentage
Yes	20	33.9
No	32	54.2
Uncertain	7	11.9
Total	59	100.0

The regret most frequently given for leaving Vietnam was separation from family members. One Vietnamese stated, "Yes, because I left many relatives, friends, and loved ones behind." Another responded, "I could not take my mother and sister along." Some who left family members behind did not know what happened to them. One household head in this predicament said, "I departed from my homeland in a state of near panic, especially after the fall of Hue. I lost contact with my parents, brothers, and sisters." Some Vietnamese missed their families and relatives and wanted to "go back to family."

Table 12

WHY

	Frequency	Percentage
Lost Relatives	13	29.6
Lost Fortune	10	22.7
Homesick, Vietnam	10	22.7
Disappointed in U.S.A.	2	4.5
Uncertain Future	4	9.1
Avoided Communists	3	6.8
Others	2	4.5
Total	44	99.9

Although some Vietnamese felt their material loss was not important, ten Vietnamese had regrets about giving up all their belongings; fortunes were left behind. One head of household put it this way, "The labor of a whole lifetime to build a good situation for the family is gone away when we left."

Ten household heads stated parting from their homeland was the reason they regretted leaving Vietnam. Phrases such as these were given, "Because Vietnam is my native land." "Left native homeland, family and fortune behind." "When finally the war is over, then we must leave our homeland for good." The deep attachment Vietnamese people have to their homeland was stated this way by one respondent, "Everybody who has to be away from his homeland would think it this way. An Oriental has always a deep bond to his homeland, much more so than a Westerner." Two respondents in this sample already are dreaming of returning to their native land: "Had to flee against my wishes. Hope one day, will have the chance to go back home." "Do not part away forever from my native land—did not expect to come to America."

Two Vietnamese heads of households indicated "disappointment with American treatment" as the reason for their regret in leaving Vietnam: "Mistreatment by the Americans—wondering whether would get reprisal from the Communists or not." "Had hoped the U.S. would treat us kindly. But it was otherwise and unexpected. Came here with nothing. Everything was lost to the Communists. Sometimes miss Vietnam because some family members are still over there." To these refugees, the price of freedom was the loss of their relatives, fortune, or homeland. As Dr. Tung, refugee Vietnamese psychiatrist, put it:

"The pain that hurts the most and will not be conquered so easily or very soon, the biggest obstacle to joy and happiness or just to normal life, is the feeling of fear and strangeness, of loneliness and helplessness when one is lost in an alien, unfamiliar world in which one has to live and adjust from now on. This had been, of course, something they tacitly submitted to since the first day they left the homeland, a nominal price to pay although they did not realize how high this price would be. And now, beyond the point of no return and for the sake of survival, they will have to see it through. . . .

"Most of the time, in spite of the conscious and unconscious efforts (to accept and conform), it hurts to live away from one's familiar world, and the required changes and adjustments are even more deeply resented because one is offered no other choice and has no way to dodge or resist—for example, by going back to one's native land (as in the case of true immigrants)."—Tung, 1975:6-7

These interviews, although at times seemingly repetitious no matter what the question was, tended to suggest that the combination of the initial circumstances, the lack of opportunities to plan, and the uncertainties in the minds of many refugees constituted a rather complex picture of the refugee's perception of the situation and their psychological fields of action. It seems there was the added reason to differentiate the situation under which flight takes place and the mechanics of flight, a point carefully presented by Kunz in his detailed typology of refugees. For example, on the dimension of forms of flight, one could do it in a group (mass flight) or as an individual. The flight could be triggered by civilian circumstances or army in flight or pursuit or separated army units after defeat. Flight might be by type of initial force (e.g., P.O.W., expellees, the forced labor, the banished, deported, or population transfers). In the case of the Vietnamese refugees, many escaped by themselves in groups, others were ordered by their superiors as in the case of former military personnel. All, however, belonged to the acute refugee category—because exit was denied or severely restricted through the erection of armed or physical barriers against exodus.

Escapes as individuals are essentially of a fragmentary nature since the size of the various groups is small. Individual or small group flights (in contrast to mass flight) are more often characterized by planned, prepared, and secret actions. Much of the Vietnamese experience consisted of the mass flights rather than individual escapes.

Also among the Vietnamese were some segments of "army in flight or pursuit," civilian evacuees, and a tendency to mass flight checked by physical barriers. There was no mass movement to evacuate all the civilians from an area, however. Some persons were displaced by "absence," such as students already in this country who decided to remain.

2
Who Are the Refugees?

We spent a lot of the taxpayer's money to help those people who are loaded with gold and American dollars, when millions are unemployed and needing federal help in this country.—An Asian-American self-portrait community worker

Demographic composition of the refugee population.—A person's response in various forms of acute displacement is governed by that person's perception of events around him, his position *vis-a-vis* the historical force, his ideological stance, sentiments, and disposition as well as his origin, age, sex, and education. Refugees, unless caused by large scale transferring of the population, seemed to be selective in terms of age and sex. Specifically, most refugees tend to be young males, with above average education.

Basic data is available on 124,457 refugees out of a total of 128,110 resettled in the United States (588 were resettled in third countries, 2,050 repatriated or wanted to be, and there were 1,807 American citizens or permanent resident aliens not included in these statistics.) There are slightly more males than females, 54.0 percent to 45.3 percent, the discrepancy being greatest in the 18-34 young adult groups. (See Table 13.) It is impossible to tell if the difference in that group can be attributed to males from army units, as compared to any sex disparity in civilian groups, either those who were evacuated systematically or those who forged their own escape. Given the usual pattern, it seems that individual escapees are high proportion male, and where civilian evacuation is keyed to the social or occupational status of the male, not a mass evacuation, the sex ratio is surprisingly balanced.

Table 13

DEMOGRAPHIC DATA

BASED ON A SAMPLE OF 124,457 REFUGEES OF WHOM

123,301 PROVIDED RELIABLE AGE INFORMATION

AGE AND SEX DISTRIBUTION

Age	Male		Female		Total	
0-5	10,572	8.6%	9,817	8.0%	20,389	16.6
6-11	9,704	7.9	8,611	7.0	18,315	14.9
12-17	9,519	7.7	8,296	6.7	17,815	14.4
18-24	13,591	11.0	9,105	7.4	22,696	18.4
25-34	12,063	9.8	8,821	7.2	20,884	17.0
35-44	6,364	5.1	5,068	4.1	11,432	9.2
45-62	4,706	3.8	4,569	3.7	9,275	7.5
63 & Over	980	.8	1,515	1.2	2,495	2.0
Total	67,499	54.7	55,802	45.3	123,301	100.0

This tells something about the strength of the Vietnamese family unit. Males apparently made enormous effort to get their families out or to arrange their escape rather than desert them. The large number of children and young people attested to this fact—45.9 percent of the total refugee population was under seventeen, mostly children of the adult refugees. It required considerable effort to secure escape for women and children and was very atypical of flight patterns under hasty and traumatic circumstances such as the closing days of the South Vietnam regime. Dr. Tung has made the same observation:

"It is common knowledge that most Vietnamese refugees had arrived with a patriarchal, large-size household from five to twelve members, and including, besides the core family, the grandparents plus some siblings, their families, and even some in-laws. The fact is most remarkable when one thinks of the immense difficulties and the numerous dangers of the precipitous escape and of the fact that all have been duly impressed with the difficulties of living in the U.S.A. with a large-size family."—Tung, 1975b:8

Table 14 on "Family Size of Indochina Evacuees up to early August" is based on a total of 24,522 families, 14,661 remaining in camp and 9,861 released from camp. It suggests that while ap-

Table 14

FAMILY SIZE OF INDOCHINA EVACUEES

Source: IATF 8/4/75

FAMILY SIZE*	REMAINING IN CAMP		RELEASED FROM CAMP		TOTAL FAMILIES	
	Numbers	Percentages**	Number	Percentages**	Numbers	Percentage
1	8,814	33	3,213	33	8,027	32.73
2	1,493	10	1,069	11	2,562	10.45
3	1,332	9	960	10	2,292	9.35
4	1,256	9	956	10	2,212	9.02
5-6	2,260	15	1,631	17	3,891	15.87
7-8	1,659	11	1,033	10	2,692	10.98
9-10	1,026	7	489	5	1,515	6.18
10	692	5	427	4	1,119	4.56
No Response	129	1	83	1	212	.86
Total	14,661	100	9,861	100	24,522	100.0

*Includes "extended" families

**Rounded Percentages

Source: from DHEW, 1975, p. 13.

proximately one third of the refugees were single individuals, 37.6 percent consisted of families of five or more members, 5 percent with more than ten members. Five to six was the model family size exclusive of single individuals.

The tendency of the Vietnamese to flee in family groups also is apparent from the Camp Pendleton data as shown in Table 15. Sixty out of 202 interviewed were heads of households, 37 spouses, 49 children, 8 mothers, 25 siblings, so that 146 were included in the immediate families. Twenty-five more were siblings of heads of households.

Table 15

RESPONDENT'S RELATIONSHIP TO HEAD OF HOUSEHOLD

Heads of Households	60	29.7
Spouse	37	18.3
Son	37	13.4
Daughter	33	10.9
Son-in-law	1	.5
Daughter-in-law	1	.5
Father	3	1.5
Mother	8	4.0
Brother	13	6.4
Sister	12	5.9
Spouse's Brother	2	1.0
Spouse's Sister	6	3.0
Nephew	3	1.5
Niece	4	2.0
Other Relatives	2	1.0
No Answer	1	0.5
Total	202	100.0

Source: Sample Survey

This might seem peculiar, given our cultural bias, but this phenomenon may represent an expedient way to handle a relative who wanted to evacuate. On the other hand, Vietnamese have large families. The size of the Vietnamese family, as shown in the sample, ranged from two to twenty-nine individuals with a median family size of 6.7. (See Table 16.)

Heads of households often considered younger siblings, cousins, and in-laws as part of the family. (In San Diego one Vietnamese refugee family had thirty-one members.) The Vietnamese people live as an extended family and reinforce kinship ties. One indica-

Returning to the age composition of the refugee population, the 45.9 percent child-refugees presented a resettlement problem of some magnitude, since only 29 percent were adult males of working age. Of course, the 14.4 percent in the twelve to seventeen age group soon would be available for work if they did not engage in further education. It was also possible that many of the adult females (22.4 percent) would start working soon after they were sponsored out, if there was suitable employment.

Very few older people were included among the refugees, suggesting that grandparents in three-generation families must be relatively young or that the perception of the presence of grandparents must be exaggerated. Statistics for the entire refugee population indicate that 64 percent of the refugee population were under twenty-five and 91.5 percent were under forty-five. (IATF, 1975b, Annex, p. 11.)

The common sense prediction that employable, younger age groups predominated among refugees was true except for the large numbers of children. Children perhaps provided a motive for flight, judging from some comments of the refugees and the efforts of parents to get their children out of Vietnam through Operation Baby Lift (Zigler, 1976) or in the general refugee exodus. Some of the unaccompanied (by adult relatives) children were commissioned by their parents or adult relatives to go alone to freedom to seek their safety and a promising future. The absence of persons in the upper thirties to sixties (16.7 percent male and 7.8 percent female) was striking. Demographically, half the population of South Vietnam was under fifteen (Zigler, 1976). Therefore, the refugee population was representative of the total population. In any event, the data suggests that flight appealed more to persons with their future before them than to persons in late middle age with more to lose; or perhaps these people were less physically adept hence less successful in escaping.

Refugees are believed to have higher average educational attainment than the population they come from. Such seems to be the case when the IATF in its concluding report examined highest educational levels of 30,628 heads of households and 67,033 other evacuees eighteen and over. (See Table 18.) 74.2 percent of the heads of households had at least some secondary education, while 27.4 percent had university or postgraduate training. Corresponding figures for all evacuees eighteen or over showed 57.4

percent secondary and 19.5 university or post-graduate, slightly lower than heads of households figures who presumably were mostly mature males. (IATF, 1975b, Annex p. 12)

Table 18

EDUCATIONAL LEVELS

Highest Educational Level of 30,628 Heads of Household

(Based on sample of 124,457 people)

	Frequency	Percentage
None	407	1.3
Elementary	5,120	16.7
Secondary	14,632	47.8
University	7,004	22.9
Post-graduate	1,375	4.5
Data not available	2,090	6.8
Total	30,628	100.0

Highest Educational Level of 67,033 Evacuees 18 Years of Age and Over

(Based on sample of 124,457 people)

	Frequency	Percentage
None	1,384	21.
Elementary	11,979	17.9
Secondary	25,432	37.9
University	11,150	16.6
Post-graduate	1,955	2.9
Data not available	15,133	22.6
Total	67,033	100.0

Source: IATF, 1975b. Annex, p. 12.

Primary employment skills surveyed support this view of a relatively high educational level. (See Table 19.) Of the heads of households, 7.2 percent were in the medical professions, plus 24 percent professional, technical, and managerial, for a total 31.2 percent professional, managerial, and technical. Few (4.9 percent) were in farming, fishing, forestry, etc. Many of the blue collar workers were skilled.

In terms of language skills, of the 30,628 heads of households, 36.7 percent had good English skills, 35.5 percent some, 27.1

percent none. Of the total refugee population, 64.7 percent reported none, 21.0 percent some, and only 13.9 percent good.

Table 19

PRIMARY EMPLOYMENT SKILLS OF

30,628 HEADS OF HOUSEHOLDS

(Based on sample of 124,457 records)

	Frequency	Percentage
Medical Professions	2,210	7.2
Professional, technical and managerial	7,368	24.0
Clerical and sales	3,572	11.7
Service	2,324	7.6
Farming, fishing, forestry and related	1,491	4.9
Agricultural processing	128	0.4
Machine trades	2,670	8.7
Benchwork, assembly and repair	1,249	4.1
Structural and construction	2,026	6.6
Transportation and miscellaneous	5,165	16.9
Did not indicate	2,425	7.9
Total	30,628	100.0

Source: IATF, 1975b, Annex p. 12.

Presumably many of these were young children who could acquire the English language more easily than refugee adults. (See Table 20.)

Data is available from several other sources on these matters. Data from the First Wave Report (a telephone survey of a sample of 1,570 heads of households representing 9,264 refugees of the first 35,000 resettled) indicates that 78.7 percent of heads of households had white collar occupations in Vietnam. Of this group (and it must be remembered, one-third were children under fourteen), one out of ten had a university degree and one out of four held the Bacc I and Bacc II secondary degrees. These two parts of completion of secondary school are the main criteria for selection of candidates for mid-level positions in the government, while Bacc II is required for university admission. Approximately 17 percent of those between six and sixty-five years of age were proficient in English, 58 percent had some knowledge, the remainder had no knowledge of English at all. (IATF, 1975a. p. 8)

Table 20

ENGLISH LANGUAGE SKILLS

30,628 Heads of Households

(Based on samples of 124,457 people)

	Frequency	Percentage
None	8,293	27.1
Some	10,867	35.5
Good	11,245	36.7
Native	223	0.7
Total	30,628	100.0

124,457 Refugees

	Frequency	Percentage
None	80,484	64.7
Some	26,205	21.0
Good	17,277	13.9
Native	491	0.4
Total	124,457	100.0

Source: IATF, 1975b, Annex, p. 14.

We can include here also the demographic data from the Camp Pendleton survey. Beginning with the basic demographic attributes of sex and age, the 202 respondents included 100 males and 102 females over thirteen years of age. The age distribution for the 202 respondents ranged from thirteen to seventy-three, with a median age of twenty-six. (See Table 21.) In reality, however, there were more than 202 people in the 59 families interviewed. The total 202 interviews included only those thirteen years of age and older.

In terms of age distribution, the median age of heads of households was approximately thirty-seven years, while that of the 202 respondents was twenty-six years. If we also consider those children under thirteen years of age who were not interviewed, the median age of the total sample would be even lower; undoubtedly the Vietnamese refugees are a young population. In our present sample, out of the 202 respondents, only seven were sixty years or older, while seventy-one were between the ages thirteen and twenty-one. Ninety percent of our respondents were under fifty years old; thus they were, or soon would be, eligible for inclusion in the labor force.

Table 21

AGE DISTRIBUTION OF ALL RESPONDENTS IN THE PRESENT SAMPLE
(OVER 13 YEARS OLD ONLY)

	Frequency	Percentage	Cumulative Percentage
13 to 14 years old	15	7.5	7.5
15 to 19	46	22.9	30.2
20 to 24	34	17.0	47.0
25 to 29	16	8.0	55.0
30 to 34	16	8.0	62.9
35 to 39	20	10.0	72.8
40 to 44	17	8.5	81.2
45 to 49	18	9.0	90.1
50 to 54	10	5.0	95.0
55 to 59	3	1.5	96.5
60 to 64	2	1.0	97.5
65 and over	5	2.5	100.0
Total	202	100.0	100.0

Source: Sample Survey

Table 22

SEX OF HEADS OF HOUSEHOLD

	Frequency	Percentage
Male	47	79.3
Female	12	20.3
Total	59	100.0

By using the usual indicators to measure socio-economic status, the survey results suggest that refugees were a select group among the Vietnamese population. The median monthly expenditure for the fifty-nine families was fifty thousand piasters. (See Table 24.)

While it is extremely difficult to interpret this value due to inflation, at the time Thieu's government fell, monthly consumption for the country as a whole was no more than ten thousand piasters. Apparently the sample refugee families would belong at least to the "upper-middle-class" equivalent of the Vietnamese society.

Table **23**

AGE DISTRIBUTION OF HEADS OF HOUSEHOLDS

	Frequency	Percentage	Cumulative Percentage
15 to 19 years old	2	3.4	3.4
20 to 24	6	10.2	13.6
25 to 29	9	15.3	28.8
30 to 34	7	11.9	40.7
35 to 39	9	15.3	55.9
40 to 44	11	18.6	76.4
45 to 49	7	11.9	86.4
50 to 54	6	10.2	96.6
55 to 59	2	3.4	100.0
Total	59	100.0	100.0

Table 24

MONTHLY HOUSEHOLD CONSUMPTION

"About how much money (in piasters) did you spend, on the the average, to cover your family living expenses for a month?" (This question was asked only of heads of households.)

	Frequency	Percentage	Cumulative Percentage
1,500 piasters or less	1	1.7	1.7
10,001 to 15,000	1	1.7	3.5
15,001 to 25,000	3	5.1	8.8
25,001 to 50,000	22	37.3	47.4
50,001 to 75,000	9	15.3	63.2
75,001 to 100,000	8	13.6	77.2
100,001 to 150,000	5	8.5	86.0
150,001 to 250,000	5	8.5	94.7
over 250,000	3	5.1	100.00
Don't know	1	------	------
No answer	1	------	------
Total	59	100.00	100.00

Source: Sample Survey

Modern conveniences were enjoyed by many Vietnamese included in this sample. (See Table 25.) There were 74.6 percent who owned a television, 78.0 percent owned a refrigerator, and 81.4 percent owned a sewing machine. The typical modes of travel were bicycle, motorbike, and car. There were 62.7 percent who owned bicycles and 76.3 percent who owned motorbikes. Cars were enjoyed by 42.4 percent of this group, with 10 percent having more than one car.

Table 25

ITEMS OWNED BY OCCUPANTS IN THE HOUSE

	Frequency	Percentage
Bicycle	37	62.7
Motorbike	45	76.3
Car	19	32.2
More than one car	6	10.2
Television	44	74.6
Refrigerator	46	78.0
Air Conditioner	15	25.4
Sewing Machine	48	81.4

Source: Sample Survey

The educational level of the heads of households is not as exceptional as their income. Twenty-one percent completed grade school, 17.5 percent completed some high school, 36.8 percent completed high school, and 15.8 percent completed some college. (See Table 26.) About half of this group had some high school with the median educational level attained approximately tenth grade.

Table 26

EDUCATIONAL LEVEL OF HEADS OF HOUSEHOLDS

	Frequency	Percentage
No formal education	2	3.5
Some elementary school	1	1.8
Finished grade school	12	21.1
Some high school	10	17.5
Finished high school	21	36.8
Vocational school	1	1.8
Some college	9	15.8
Graduate school	1	1.8
No answer	1	----
Total	59	100.0%

Source: Sample Survey

According to the heads of households own ratings, forty or seventy percent could converse in English. (See Table 27.) Twenty-two percent rated themselves as speaking fluently and 47.4 percent with some fluency. About one-third could not speak English. Written English could be understood by 17.5 percent.

Forty-two percent of the Vietnamese heads of households could speak French. Fourteen percent spoke fluently and 28.1 percent with some fluency. Proficiency in Chinese was acknowledged by 7 percent of the Vietnamese heads of households.

In terms of occupations, though, the sample heads of households were clearly a select group. (See Table 28.) Out of the fifty-nine heads of households, twenty were in the Armed Forces of the South Vietnamese government, five were in Civil Service, and another five were employed by the Americans. Other heads of households were employed in a wide variety of occupations— professionals, businessmen, fishermen, farmers, housewives, students.

Of the same sample of 202 respondents, eighty-four or 41.6 percent were not employed in Vietnam. This number includes 11 percent or twenty-one children under sixteen years of age, 19.4 percent or thirty-seven students, 8.9 percent or seventeen housewives, and 4.7 percent or nine non-workers. (See Table 29.) Most of the Vietnamese could tell the interviewer the last steady job they held in Vietnam but could not tell how they obtained the job. Thirty-four were self-employed and owned a variety of businesses such as grocery stores, restaurants, dressmaker shops, textile weaving shops, wood product shops, and fishing companies. The self-employed farmed, ranched, or sold products such as rice, cosmetics, and clothes.

The Vietnamese obtained their last job in several ways, by (1) volunteer or draft into military service, (2) applying and passing test, (3) help from friends or relatives, (4) assignment, and (5) selection. Those who applied and got jobs on their own included job occupations such as fraud agent with customs and assistant manager for a pharmaceutical company. Others applied but also needed to pass tests for their jobs as policemen, health technicians, agricultural engineers, and English typists.

Friends or relatives assisted some Vietnamese in finding employment in the Embassy, on Advertising Weekly Magazine staff, and as a painter. Other Vietnamese were selected or pro-

Table 27

LANGUAGE PROFICIENCY OF HEADS OF HOUSEHOLDS

	Frequency	Percentage	Frequency	Percentage	Frequency	Percentage
Fluent	13	22.8	8	14	2	3.5
Not fluent	27	47.4	16	28.1	2	3.5
Not spoken	10	17.5	13	22.8	21	36.8
Not at all	7	12.3	20	35.1	32	56.1
No answer	2		2		2	
Total	59	100.0	59	100.0	59	100.0

Source: Sample Survey

Source: Mineta, 1975

Table **28**

OCCUPATIONS OF THE HEADS OF HOUSEHOLDS

Occupation	Frequency	Percentage
Military, Army	3	5.2
Military, Navy	4	6.9
Special Forces	3	5.2
Police	3	5.2
Civil Service	2	3.4
US Employee	2	3.4
Professional	3	5.2
Teacher	1	1.7
Manager	1	1.7
Businessperson	3	5.2
Owner	1	1.7
Small Business	2	3.4
Skilled Worker	5	8.6
Fisherman	3	5.2
Farmer, Rancher	1	1.7
Secretary	2	3.4
Seamstress	2	3.4
Housewife	2	3.4
Student	4	6.9
Others	2	3.4
Total	59	100.0

Source: Sample Survey

Table **29**

WAY RESPONDENT GOT HIS LAST JOB IN VIETNAM

	Frequency	Percentage
ArVN Drafted	6	3.1
ArVN Volunteer	4	2.1
Self-employed	34	17.8
Student	37	19.4
Housewife	17	8.9
Employed by US	1	.5
Applied for the Job	16	8.4
Through Friends	5	2.6
Did Not Work	9	4.07
Under 16	21	11.0
Selected to do Job	1	11.5
Others	40	20.9
No Answer	11	-----
Total	202	100.0

Source: Sample Survey

moted to better positions such as editor for the U.S. Embassy, head of the Regional Security Police, and head of the Open Arm Program.

As shown in Table 30, all the respondents were born in Vietnam. Forty-three percent or eighty-seven respondents were born north of the 17th Parallel and one-hundred and twelve or 55 percent were born south of the 17th Parallel. All those born north of the 17th Parallel had migrated to South Vietnam prior to 1975. Previous to 1954, 59 percent of the heads of households lived in North Vietnam. The older the respondents, the more likely they were born in the north and migrated south; this suggests that the older generation had already experienced a previous refugee flight in 1954. They previously had experienced fleeing from Communist rule. One former serviceman stated, "We are not of the same political beliefs, so we ran away from the Communists in 1954." A similar statement: "We fear the Communists because we fled North Vietnam and worked for the U.S. embassy in Saigon."

Table 30

LOCATION OF BIRTH

	Frequency	Percentage
North of 17th Parallel	87	43.1
South of 17th Parallel	112	55.4
No answer	3	1.5
Total	202	100.0

Source: Sample Survey

Prior to 1975, 195 or 96.5 percent of this Vietnamese sample had never resided outside of Vietnam. (See Table 31.) Only five respondents resided in another country. Three of this sample lived in two different countries. The foreign countries of residence were France, Morocco, and Laos. Vietnam was their permanent home. About half or 49 percent of the heads of households reported living in Saigon, and another 21 percent reported living in a city previous to coming to the United States. This makes 70 percent of the people urban dwellers as compared to only 5 percent from the countryside setting.

Table 31

DID RESPONDENT LIVE SOMEWHERE ELSE PRIOR TO 1975?

	Frequency	Percentage
Yes	5	2.5
No	195	96.5
No answer	2	1.0
Total	202	100.0

Survey: Sample Survey

Table 32

PERMANENT HOME IN VIETNAM

Location	Frequency	Percentage
Province	12	21.1
City	12	21.1
Countryside	3	5.3
Saigon	28	49.1
Other	2	3.5
No Answer	2	----
Total	59	100.0

Source: Sample Survey

Table 33

IMPORTANCE OF RELIGION

	Frequency	Percentage
Extremely important	111	55.2
Very important	41	20.4
Moderately important	30	14.9
Not so important	15	7.5
Not important at all	5	2.0
No Answer	1	----
Total	202	100.0

Source: Sample Survey

There were 55.2 percent or 111 Vietnames who felt religion was of 100 percent importance to them. (See Table 33.) Only 10 percent of the Vietnamese felt religion was of little or no importance to them.

The majority or 55 percent of this Vietnamese sample were Catholics, 27.2 percent Buddhists and 10.9 percent Confucians. (See Table 34.) Only 5 percent reported having no religion. There was almost an even distribution between those who practiced and did not practice ancestor worship. Typically, Catholics did not follow ancestor worship while non-Catholics did.

Table 34

RELIGIOUS BELIEF

	Frequency	Percentage
Buddhist	55	27.2
Catholic	111	55.0
Protestant	1	.5
Confucian	22	10.9
Other	1	.5
None	10	5.0
More than one religion	2	1.0
Total	202	100.0

Source: Sample Survey

Table 35

DO YOU PRACTICE ANCESTOR WORSHIP?

	Frequency	Percentage
Yes	92	46.9
No	104	53.1
No answer	6	----
Total	202	100.0

Source: Sample Survey

Thus the Vietnamese refugees by all accounts were a young, relatively well-educated and skilled segment of the population. From this point of view, they were desirable immigrants. From the point of view of the refugees themselves, the same description means that considerable status deprivation was experienced by the refugees in migrating both in terms of future occupational opportunities and in terms of social positions after their resettlement. Any prejudice manifested against Asians would add to the sense of status loss. These Vietnamese were not at all voluntary migrants who expected to improve their socio-economic situation. The Vietnamese refugees were persons who were pushed out of their niche by perceived threats to personal safety, some acting with forethought, others with little warning or planning, others entirely accidentally. This is a difficult psychological situation. They came in family groups somewhat more extensive and balanced than would be perceived by Kunz's refugee theory (Kunz, 1973).

3
Reactions of the American Public

Damn it, we have too many Orientals already. If they all gravitate to California, the tax and welfare rolls will get overburdened and we already have our share of the illegal aliens.—Former Representative Burt Talcott (R. Calif.)

The refugees, in a certain sense and from their point of view, could be considered reluctant entrants into refugee status. From the point of view of the public in the host country, heroic as the evacuation episode was, it seemed to be overwhelmed by the more practical considerations of resettling the refugees within the United States. Actually, even before they came, opinions were harsh and unfavorable to the incoming of refugees, especially in California where most were expected to stay. Rumors flourished. About one million refugees were expected to flood into California. Governor Brown declared, "We can't be looking five thousand miles away and at the same time neglecting people who are living here" (*U.S. News and World Report*, May 15, 1975, p. 22). An Arkansas woman said: "They say it's a lot colder here than in Vietnam. With a little luck, maybe all those Vietnamese will take pneumonia and die" (*Newsweek*, May 12, 1975, p. 32). Senator McGovern also expressed his view: "Ninety percent of the Vietnamese refugees would be better off going back to their own land" (*Time*, May 19, 1975, p. 9).

The Gallup Poll taken in early May showed that "fifty-four percent of all Americans (were) opposed to admitting Vietnamese refugees to live in the United States and only 36 percent (were) in favor" (*Time*, May 19, 1975, p. 9).

And in an act of collective decision, the House voted 246-162 against the bill authorizing $327 million in humanitarian aid for the Vietnamese refugees (*New York Times*, May 2, 1975). Consequently President Ford was "damned mad" about such widespread opposition to resettlement of the refugees because, in his words, "we are a country built by immigrants . . . and we have always been a humanitarian nation" (*U.S. News and World Report*, May 19, 1975, p. 1). In spite of the President's appeal, newspapers in southern California early in June printed stories about the first Vietnamese family receiving welfare checks.

But not all Americans were unresponsive. The AFL-CIO Executive Board passed a resolution urging that the refugees be welcomed, that their presence in the job market hardly would be significant. Voluntary organizations such as the Red Cross, the International Rescue Committee, the United States Catholic Conference, Lutheran World Relief, and the United HIAS were extremely active in sponsoring the refugees. Some American companies who had employees in Vietnam—IBM, Chase Manhattan Bank, New York Times—promised to place their former employees within their organizations (*Newsweek*, May 19, p. 74). And the editorial standpoints of the major newspapers and magazines such as *Time*, *Newsweek*, the *New York Times*, and the *Los Angeles Times*, consistently endorsed President Ford's position regarding resettlement. Much of the initial negative reaction of the Americans against the refugees was bred in an atmosphere of rumors, economic self-interest, guilt reactions, and racism. Much to the credit of President Ford's appeal and the mass media's advocacy, the cold reception soon was replaced by a more positive attitude. The Congress on May 14 approved a $405 million bill to fund resettlement programs, and President Ford signed the bill into law ten days later.

On May 1, the White House announced the formation of the President's Advisory Committee on Refugees with John Eisenhower selected as chairman. Some of the voluntary organizations involved in the resettlement of refugees thus far were represented. However, the list of seventeen names did not contain one single Asian, though at least two names were submitted to the White House for consideration.

The reception on the part of the official government agencies seemed to be less than what was expected by the Congress. Throughout the first two weeks in April, thirteen federal agencies were involved in the coordination of refugee resettlement.

Since not enough time was allowed to plan the operation, at the beginning each of these agencies operated independently of each other and occasionally in conflict with each other (Mineta *et al*, 1975).

Despite the humanitarian concerns this country is noted for, a simplistic and altogether too "efficient" operation to get rid of the refugee problem quickly and to close the camps exposes a less favorable side of the entire program. The protection of extremely vulnerable civilian Vietnamese population and military personnel from possible punishment by the Communist regime was not a problem of recent vintage but had existed for at least a decade. Why had there been no planning for the mass evacuation and no preparation for the reception of evacuees after a long and bitter war? The token gesture of having more than one hundred thousand Vietnamese brought over on such short notice without any coordination and effort on the local community level to resettle these people made our country vulnerable to charges of racism and inefficiency. For example, on the tragic handling of the Baby Airlift project, Zigler commented:

"Furthermore, as I read through the grey prose of countless memoranda issued by federal officials in regard to the social services needs of the Vietnamese, it became apparent to me that while these officials were dedicated, they were part of a bureaucracy that had become too cumbersome and ponderous to be able to proceed with a task quickly, decisively, and well."—Zigler, 1975:4

Zigler's comment, especially the last sentence, pinpointed the mentality of the civilian coordinator at Camp Pendleton, and, to a greater extent, the mentality of the highest civilian authority in charge of the entire refugee operation in Washington. They were more concerned with the discharge statistics than the welfare and fate of hundreds upon thousands of refugees in the initial contact with a country they had had no option to choose.

Meanwhile, elsewhere in the nation, a Louis Harris poll in June showed that 49 percent opposed and only 37 percent accepted immigration of the Vietnamese refugees. A second poll conducted in August 1977 showed virtually no change in the public acceptance of refugees after two years. Objection was principally the anticipated strain on our unemployment rate—62 percent believed the immigrants would take jobs away from Americans.

Objectors also believed (a rationalization) that the U.S. overestimated the desire of the refugees to come to America, 85 percent believed there was too much panic about rescuing refugees and felt the United States should arrange to aid those who wanted to return. (Reporters, however, found little sentiment among the Vietnamese against being rescued, and few ultimately elected to be repatriated.) Strangely enough, while people in all regions opposed permanent resettlement of the Vietnamese in the United States, the heaviest opposition was from southerners. They had been most hawkish in supporting the war and now joined skilled workers, anticipating job problems. The only groups who supported the acceptance of the Vietnamese were the college educated (48 percent to 39 percent) and the professionals (53 percent to 32 percent). Those groups who had been most opposed to the war itself and to last minute military aid for the Saigon regime were willing to accept the refugees. (L. Harris, 1975)

The reaction of those bureaucrats immediately concerned with the problem was to delay and limit entry into refugee status and to process refugees out of refugee status as soon as possible. The welcome extended to the refugees was thus a tentative one. As Dr. Tung comments:

"In this particular group of refugees, because they came in the wake of an unpopular war and in the midst of internal difficulties, the sentiment is that of confusion, even of humiliation, as if they were some self-invited guests who fear they are perhaps imposing upon a host whose intentions are not too clear."— Tung, 1975b:6

The following points can be made to indicate the limited welcome, i.e. limited entry into refugee status permitted by the host country, in spite of President Ford's statement of ethical responsibility to those who had collaborated with the Americans or were otherwise vulnerable:

1) Planning was late and insufficient so that persons in eligible categories were physically unable to escape.

2) Entry into refugee status was limited in terms of overall numbers to 75,000 relatives and 50,000 other high-risk Vietnamese. In this case, as well as the preceding, a considerable number of ineligible persons were able to become refugees and

were received by the United States. The overall total, however, did not encompass more than projected.

3) As noted above, funds were first refused by Congress, before being appropriated. The Indochina Migration and Refugee Assistance Act (P.L. 94-23) was signed into law by President Ford on May 23, 1975 (the refugees began arriving in April); it provided $305 million to the Department of State and related agencies for evacuating and resettling the refugees and another $100 million to the Department of Health Education and Welfare to pay for health, education, and welfare services for the Vietnamese and Cambodians; this compares with $584 million for the Cubans (*U.S. News*, May 5, p. 23). Funding was thus less than what might have been expected, certainly less than needed.

4) The climate of public opinion was somewhat hostile, though editorial support for humanitarian efforts on behalf of the refugees was forthcoming.

The major argument against accepting the Vietnamese refugees concerned displacement of Americans in their jobs. If the Vietnamese were to resettle en masse in areas such as southern California, Florida, Texas, or New York, the strain in local unemployment could be extremely unpleasant. But the Ford Administration had promised to resettle the refugees as diversely as possible. (*N.Y. Times*, April 25, 1:5). From a purely economic viewpoint, the infusion of human resources of such magnitude should prove beneficial to the U.S. economy. As Paul Samuelson so eloquently phrased it, "A society that had no need for such people is not so much to be envied as pitied" (*Newsweek*, May 26, p. 71). The addition of ten thousand Vietnamese auto mechanics in the Detroit area would be riotous, but 35,000 job seekers in an economy that has millions in the work force is practically negligible.

The second line of argument pertained to the huge amount of monies thought to be necessary in order to resettle the refugees. The President had within his authority $405 million to be spent for evacuation and humanitarian needs within the first eighteen months of the resettlement. These funds included reimbursing all state and local expenditures for the refugees, thereby assuaging much of the furor raised by local communities, especially those near the camps. And while the $405 million may seem a huge sum at first, it is miniscule compared to the $140 billion that had been fueled into the Vietnam War. Even more to the point, if the United States invested $583 million in the Cuban refugees (*U.S. News*, May 5, p. 23), spending the $405 million seems equally legitimate.

Another point crucial to this issue, but often ignored, is the dividend on the investment. Samuelson already alluded to the richness of these human resources. Among the refugees were approximately five hundred physicians, according to the HEW's latest estimate. To take a concrete historical precedent, in 1948 when President Truman signed into law The Displaced Persons Act (see *The DP Story*, The US Government Printing Press, 1952), he commissioned a program that was eventually to bring in some four hundred thousand refugees, mostly of European origin. In the opinion of the Displaced Persons Commission, it was "a good investment" because those people repaid in one year in Federal income taxes three times the total cost of the operation. (To be more exact, $57 million compared to $19 million; see p. 350 of the report.) Historically, refugees as a group always have been decent and honest working people. They might require help and funding to get started, but eventually they establish themselves. Perhaps they have come to treasure more than the native-born Americans the fundamental tenets of this nation: freedom, equality, and the pursuit of happiness.

There were intimations of anti-Oriental prejudice reflected in some of the earlier quotations, satirized by Art Buchwald in a column on the symbolic significance of the Statue of Liberty facing east to Europe. Just as the United States, in 1976, had two hundred years of democracy to commemorate, it also unfortunately had inherited an ugly racist legacy. "Charity begins at home," said one protest sign; "Only Ford wants them," said another (*Time*, May 12, p. 15).

Resettlement of the Vietnamese seemed to be contingent on dispersal so there would be no concentrations to prove an economic or racial threat. Whether this was best for the adjustment of the Vietnamese will be discussed later. Congressman Mineta's report showed some concern about the burden which might be cast upon particular localities, California in particular. (Mineta, et.al. 1975)

Congressman Mineta concluded, "I believe that now the refugees are in the United States, we should provide them with the necessary assistance," but expressed some concern as "a member of Congress from the State of California—a state which is expected to receive approximately 23 percent of the total refugee population" (Mineta, *et. al.* p. 1). He also referred to the Ford administration's indication that the Federal government would provide the necessary support to protect local communities from any adverse impacts of refugee resettlement in terms of burdens on schools, welfare rolls, health services, and job markets. The positive effects of these assurances on public attitudes was noted by Mineta (p. 34). The funds appropriated by the federal government included reimbursing all state and local expenditures for the refugees. Mineta was critical of the extent of reimbursement to school systems, as well as the overall comprehensiveness and effort, from the viewpoint of the refugees as well as the impact on local communities.

One of the most detrimental aspects of a sudden refugee exodus such as the Vietnamese experienced is the sharp rupture of the social fabric—familial and community ties and a familiar culture. By depriving the Vietnamese of this social support, we freed them to undertake a much more difficult readjustment than previous refugees or even voluntary migrants.

We must note, though, that adoption of a scattered resettlement policy (in response to political pressure and public opinion) may prove detrimental to the successful resettlement and the mental health of the refugees. Previous refugee groups, the Cubans for example, have derived considerable psychological support as well as material help and counsel from the presence of others of their culture.

Finally, as noted above, there may have been undue haste in processing Vietnamese out of the camp and lack of concern with follow-up. Examples of this are the setting of a deadline far in advance for closing the camps, pressure to empty camps on schedule, and the tendency to accept unsuitable arrangements. For example, the "group sponsorship" toward the end of the "reception period," or the decision concerning "unaccompanied" children who were placed in hastily arranged foster home plans with parents who had no sensitivity to the cultural differences between their own family rituals and the customary ways of these children.

In sum, refugee status and the obligations incurred are defined by both the receiving country and the refugees. The host country, in this case, the United States, attempted (1) to limit entry into refugee status or at least not to facilitate a great number of refugees, and (2) to limit duration and extensiveness in terms of claims on resources of refugee status. In response there was (1) circumvention by refugees who managed to create their entry into the refugee stream, then acceptance by the host country; and (2) opposition by refugees—and their advocates—to aspects of resettlement which reduced government and private agency responsibility; the refugees could not view resettlement as their own responsibility since they had come to the host country in reaction to events—not on their own initiative as voluntary migrants.

Definition of refugee status and its temporal extent, such as timing and transition through the various career stages, was thus a matter of negotiation, conflict, and circumvention in which expectations of neither the refugee nor the host community were completely realized.

The symbolic burden of the Vietnamese refugee.—While quick disposition of "refugee problems" by bureaucratic fiat appears always to be with us, the Vietnamese refugees may be unique in failing to elicit their fair share of sympathy. As Kunz points out, since refugee problems are the outcome of political and military events, it is difficult for people to treat refugees objectively. For many, the refugee serves as a reminder of the war and our involvement and responsibility in the face of a predominant mood in the country to forget and obliterate the memory of this unsuccessful effort.

Zigler, in "Developmental Psychologists' View of Operation Baby Lift," points out:

"The problems of refugees and orphaned children have existed for at least ten years. Why was this lead time for careful analysis and planning lost, forcing our nation to behave in a precipitous manner that made us vulnerable to charges of racism, elitism, chauvinism, and disregard for the best interest of Vietnamese children and their families? Countless memoranda were issued by federal officials in recent years concerning the social service needs of the Vietnamese."—Zigler, 1976:329-330

He gives due credit by admitting that:

"A general impression of the Vietnamese children's airlift was that it represented what is best and worst in our nation's ethos. On the positive side, there was our characteristic sympathy for the downtrodden and generosity to those less fortunate than ourselves, phenomena that were expressed in an outpouring of volunteer labor and offers of assistance."—Zigler, 1976:324

However, the Union of Vietnamese in America called the program "kidnapping" (Zigler, 1976:330) and Joseph Reid, Executive Director of the Child Welfare League of America pointed out the great concern of Vietnamese for their children and suggested that our concern should be to help them, not to remove the children from the country.

Zigler documents some of the poor organization in this project, which perhaps was detrimental to the welfare of the children in transit. Furthermore, in terms of the total number of orphaned children, this was: "little more than a token effort, since in 1973 half of the Vietnamese population of 17-18 million was under fourteen, 880,000 at least partial orphans, 29,000 children in registered orphanages."

Zigler concluded: "Thus the airlift episode was little more than a tokenistic effort. A danger of tokenistic efforts lies in giving the appearance that a great deal is being done, which in turn interferes with moving on to more honest and realistic broad-scale efforts."

Zigler's comment is most interesting and broadly relevant to the total Vietnamese refugee program in terms of American guilt, chauvinism, and racism.

"Without question the war in Southeast Asia presented a deeply disturbing problem to the individual and collective psyches of Americans. When confronted with such problems, individuals often respond with a variety of psychological mechanisms that defend them against the anxiety aroused by threatening situations. It would be foolish to argue that there is not a sizeable group of Americans who feel considerable guilt concerning our nation's role in Vietnam and thus have engaged in or supported those actions that expiate such guilt feelings (although) . . . it would be an oversimplification to impute to all of them a common underlying guilt complex."—Zigler, 1976:333

Zigler refers also to denial, citing comments of Rep. Bonker that "people are drained. They want to bury the memory of Indochina," and the 68 percent surveyed by *Time* who believed "we should put Vietnam behind us and not worry about who was to blame."

Zigler refers to the "massive disrespect for the Vietnamese people (both South and North)" implied in Operation Babylift, which suggested the Vietnamese would not care for their children and "being raised by Americans in America was superior to being raised by Vietnamese in Vietnam."

"Americans have not paid enough attention to the fact that the Vietnamese have a culture that extends backward in time 2,000 years. Nor have we appreciated sufficiently the fact that in the Vietnamese culture there is a greater respect for the family unit than there is in America. Even with the ravages of war, the extended family, which readily takes in orphaned children, is currently more viable in Vietnam than it is in the United States. . . . To see these children removed from Vietnam, renamed with Americanized first names, and forever denied access to their native heritage and culture was insulting to many Vietnamese, whatever their political affiliations might be."—Zigler, 1976:334

"The foregoing look at Operation Babylift and the issues raised by this effort should make clear the humanitarian needs of the Vietnamese people cannot be met by bringing 2,000 Vietnamese children to America for adoption, nor by transporting a relatively small number of Vietnamese refugees to our shore. What is needed at this critical juncture of America's involvement in Vietnam is a comprehensive plan of assistance for the babylift children, for the refugees, and for the human and physical reconstruction of Vietnam . . . We must recognize . . . (the) humanitarian needs of overwhelming proportions . . . and the entire federal bureaucracy must be mobilized to fulfill them."— Zigler, 1976:335-336

Zigler's comments on the Babylift, which he extended to the refugees in general, were echoed by a journalist's comments after a visit to Camp Pendleton (Chuman, *Rafu Shimpo,* published in English language in a Japanese-American newspaper in Los Angeles May 22, 1975). He commented on the rapidity with which the camps were emptied whether or not suitable sponsors had been obtained. "If the goal is to make them vanish, so to speak, why were nearly 200,000 refugees taken out of their countries? Was it out of American humanitarianism? Or were these families shipped out of their countries to lend a little dignity to a graceless American exodus from Southeast Asia?"

In sum, criticism was made that attention and effort were channeled into token and, in this case, highly questionable efforts such as Operation Baby Lift. These were not sufficiently substantial but permitted a feeling of having cared for the Vietnamese and permitted closing the books.

In dealing with the overall American reaction, we are getting ahead of our story from the Vietnamese perspective. The next chapter will return to the story of the transit of the Vietnamese from their country to their sometimes unanticipated destination of the United States.

4
The Refugee in Transit
Midway-to-nowhere—Kunz, 1973

Trauma of transit.—Once the refugees fled Vietnam, they had to live through many uncertainties, persevere despite starvation and other material hardships, and see other people dying, including relatives. They lost their identities. They did not know where they were going. They were frightened and at a loss for points to anchor their lives. They also witnessed extreme forms of cruelty. These experiences described as the most unforgettable events hardened the old as well as the young. (See Table 36.)

Table 36

MOST UNFORGETTABLE EVENT

	Frequency	Percentage
Lack of food	23	36.5
Seeing misery and defeat	14	22.2
Lost relatives	8	12.7
Uncertainties	14	22.2
Bombing	2	3.2
Panic Scenes	2	3.2
Total	63	100.0

Source: Sample Survey

Starvation was listed most frequently as the most unforgettable event of the trip. Overcrowded conditions, hunger, suffocation, and death were experienced by many of the refugees. Vietnamese aboard the ship from Vietnamese offshore Phu Quoc Island to Subic Bay in the Philippines reported getting just one spoonful of rice per day, being hungry for twenty-four days and starving for seven days. A mother stated, "For the first time in my life I had to witness my own children starving aboard the ship." One vividly remembered the first real dinner in the Philippines. Another described an incident in Guam, "At chow time I dropped my plate. When I asked for another one, not only did I not get it, but I was almost beaten. That was the most degrading thing for Vietnamese people."

Fourteen Vietnamese were struck by the misery suffered during evacuation. "Life aboard the ship was miserable. Material life was lacking. Morale was very low. Arrival at the Guam refugee camp was sad because we went from one disappointment to another. This was due to the American evacuation methods. We were treated worse as we went along."

The sanitary conditions got worse as time progressed. "It was like living in a pig pen," according to one Vietnamese. Another individual reported being "very upset from Phu Quoc to Singapore about the seamen, because many accidents occurred as a result of them." Illness among the refugees also caused concern. "The children were seriously ill." One man reported, "During the plane trip from Saigon to Clark (Air Force Base in the Philippines) I was very worried about my mother because she was ill and unconscious."

Fourteen Vietnamese indicated that the most unforgettable event for them was the uncertainty of life. Uppermost on the minds of many Vietnamese was a way to get out of Vietnam. "I did not know whether or not I would be picked up by anybody. I had grave fear." Locating a fishing junk was difficult, but even at sea additional difficulties were encountered. Some reports of these hardships and uncertainties were described:

"I lost sense of direction, was followed by sharks at Con Son Island and then after boarding the ship, the skipper tried to take us back to the communist area."

"Our ship was under fire. Rain poured. The engine broke down. No radio. No compass. The ship just drifted aimlessly."

"We were drifting in the middle of the ocean. The ship was out of order. I was very nervous and tense. My only hope was that all go well and we get to shore. I was not able to get refueled or get food provisions."

"During the trip from Phu Quoc to Singapore I feared bad weather. The engine broke down. I did not know where to go—I was very fearful."

"We did not know whether or not we would get to our destination because the boat was too small. I was afraid of running out of fuel, the storms, and perhaps not being welcomed and thrown out (after reaching destinations)."

"Family's state of mind very low. No idea what will happen in the future."

Vietnamese refugees often witnessed death. Killings occurred along the road to the airport and harbor. Shellings were frequent. According to one eyewitness, "From Saigon to the offshore meeting with the U.S. Navy there was lots of shelling and it was very dangerous." Another reported, "Communist shellings hit many small boats on the way from the shoreline to the U.S. ships offshore. Boats caught fire." Sometimes the shellings ended in lost lives, "The ship was under fire. One child was killed and the rest of the family wounded."

Watching people die was not infrequent:

"One airborne officer committed suicide on the trip from Saigon to Subic Bay."

"Many Vietnamese Air Force pilots abandoned their planes by jumping aboard ships bound for freedom. Some pilots did not make it and were killed."

"I witnessed a helicopter attempt to land on a barge. It crashed and I thought I was going to be killed."

"I saw many junks hit by shelling sink offshore from Vung Tau."

"One ship had to tow another. The line broke away. Two men were thrown and lost at sea."

"Boat out of order with no steering and no crankshaft. Run the boat with only two engines; direction with only the star as compass. (Then) out of fuel . . . waited from 6 P.M. to 6 A.M. to be picked up."

"Ship under fire when leaving Saigon harbor. Fifteen days lay on deck of ship."

Asking refugees to recount their experiences en route to America was perhaps the most difficult part of the interview.

Quite frequently interviewers stopped the interview and talked about other things as the respondent could not continue to bear the emotional burden associated with the experience of the flight. Many tragic events were left unspoken or unfinished. However, interviewers assured them that the purpose of the interview was to keep a complete account of what happened to the refugees so that both service providers and those who would handle future events concerning refugees would have a better understanding of the emotional and cultural aspects of their ability to cope with the situation. The following may be illustrative:

Interviewer: "What was the one event during the trip you will never forget?"

Woman Respondent: "It was when all of these people were trying to get on the plane at the airport. I saw people jamming the door and women and children could not get on. The shelling came closer and then the plane took off with people still hanging at the door, and then . . . (sob)"

(After a few seconds of silence on the tape)

Interviewer: "It's all right. It is only natural. Let's take a break."

Family separations were suffered by many in the chaos of evacuation. Separation from other family members occurred as a result of the crowds jammed into Saigon harbor. "The panic of the crowd and disruption at Saigon harbor forced the MP's to fire shots into the air and use water jets to disperse and prevent civilians from entering the naval base." "It is difficult to forget the way people were fleeing in panic situations."

When boarding U.S. ships there were many instances of parents losing children and other relatives. As one person reported, "Separation is sad . . . very hard to forget these moments."

One woman had lost her child, nine years old, and her husband during evacuation. Another had no relatives on ship and travelled alone. One Vietnamese man said, "I watched my children miss their mother. They needed a motherly hand to take care of them."

Some of these separations were not permanent. A lady reported that her "son-in-law was detained at the Tan Son Nhut airport in Saigon. We had to hire people to get him out but he missed his plane connection. Because he was a permanent U.S. resident and had a job offer at a hospital in Philadelphia, he was able to show his card to the U.S. authorities and get into the base and fly out to Guam." The son-in-law reunited with his family in Pendleton three weeks later.

Feelings of sadness were felt when on ship Vietnam's colors were changed to the United States' colors. According to one report, "When the Vietnamese ship got to Subic Bay, the Vietnamese flag had to be taken down . . . everybody watched the flag going down with heartbroken feeling, knowing they will never see it raised again."

Extreme hardships were suffered by the refugees prior to their arrival in California. One Vietnamese stated: "Lost everything. I was barefoot when I arrived at camp." Mental states were quite low. And then they faced additional hostilities and suspicions from both the native population and the government. Many liberal Americans still thought all refugees were rich right wing followers of the unpopular leader of the South Vietnamese regime, Thieu.

Some recollections were happier, or at least less serious: "Happy to see the 7th fleet." "No relatives along." "Needed cigarettes." Only nine of fifty-nine heads of household interviewed remained silent.

On April 24, the first staging area was set up on Guam, with additional ones on Wake Island, Subic Bay, Clark Air Force Base in the Philippines, and Hickam Field in Hawaii. The refugees had to stop at one of the Pacific staging areas before being admitted to mainland camps. Some refugees made more than one Pacific stop and others had had several previous stops in their escape from Vietnam.

Refugee kinetics: "push-pressure"?—The transit from home in Vietnam to Camp Pendleton, in the case of the refugees interviewed, sometimes involved several transfers. Camp Pendleton refugees were asked in detail about their transit stops, mode of transportation, and advance knowledge of destination. A common pattern for this group was stops of varied duration at Subic Bay and Guam or Clark AFB and Wake Island. On the average, the refugees took eleven days to get to Pendleton and had three interim destinations. Often, the refugees did not know where they were going when they embarked on boat or plane.

Kunz points out that acute refugee movements contrast—in kinetics as well as selectiveness—with anticipatory or voluntarily motivated migration which is more apt to have a specific destination and "door-to-door transit."

The typical route for those leaving Vietnam was first to offshore Vietnamese places to get away from the desperate conditions. (See Table 38.) 47.5 percent spent an average of three days on ships or islands such as Con Son and Phu Quoc. Then, the Philippine Islands were a stopping place for 72.9 percent of the sample. The Vietnamese stayed there an average of 12.45 days. Before this stop, 22 percent of the refugees stopped in Singapore or Thailand for an average of five days. The third stop was Guam for 81.4 percent of the Vietnamese. At this most frequently used stop, the stay averaged twenty-seven days for the Vietnamese en route to Camp Pendleton. Another 23.7 percent of the refugees stopped at Wake Island for an average of seven weeks. Finally, after many days of travel, they reached Camp Pendleton.

It took an average of 50.32 days to travel from Vietnam to Camp Pendleton. (See Table 39.) The shortest amount of time was three days; the longest, 122 days. The mean number of stops from Vietnam to Camp Pendleton was four. The number of stops ranged from one to seven. (See Table 40.)

The routes taken by the Vietnamese from Vietnam to Camp Pendleton are shown in Table 37. The most frequently used route was from Vietnam to the Philippines to Guam to Camp Pendleton—44.1 percent travelled it; 18.6 percent went from Vietnam making just one stop in Guam before reaching Camp Pendleton. About 32 percent travelled to Camp Pendleton stopping in the Philippines, Guam, and Wake Island.

Although 93 percent of the sample left Vietnam between April 25 and April 30, only 20.3 percent arrived at Pendleton during May. During the months of June and July, another 67.8 percent of the Vietnamese entered Pendleton.

Asked if they knew where they were going, 67.9 percent responded *yes* and 32 percent responded *no* or *uncertain.* Their location when the Vietnamese learned their destinations is shown in Table 43. Just 27.1 percent realized where they were going when they left Vietnam. 16.9 percent found out where they were headed in Guam, and 18.6 percent knew in the Philippines. After arriving at Camp Pendleton 22.1 percent stated they either still did not know or were uncertain about where they were going.

Kunz refers to the "midway to nowhere" no-man's land before

Table 37

ROUTES TO CAMP PENDLETON

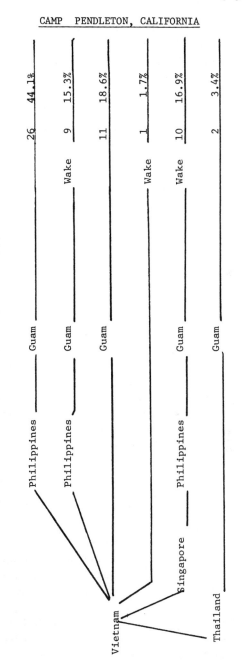

CAMP PENDLETON, CALIFORNIA

Vietnam	Philippines	Guam	26	44.1%
Vietnam	Philippines	Guam	Wake	9	15.3%
Vietnam		Guam	11	18.6%
Vietnam			Wake	1	1.7%
Vietnam — Singapore	Philippines	Guam	Wake	10	16.9%
Vietnam — Thailand		Guam	2	3.4%

Source: Sample Survey

Table 38

STOP-OVER POINTS EN ROUTE TO CAMP PENDLETON

	Frequency	Percentage
Vietnam		100.0
1 stop	14	23.7
2 stops	8	13.6
Saigon	18	30.5
Off Shore Vietnam	28	47.5
Islands		
Ships		
Singapore	11	18.6
Thailand	2	3.4
Philippine Islands	43	72.9
Guam	48	81.4
Wake Island	14	23.7
Asan Camp	1	1.7
Hawaii	1	1.7
Anderson Base, Cal.	2	3.4
Camp Pendleton	59	100.0

Source: Sample Survey

Table 39

LENGTH OF STAY AT EACH STOP

	Range	Mean
Offshore Vietnam	less than 12 hrs to 4 weeks	4.38 days
Singapore	2 days – 1 week	4.55 days
Thailand	3 days – 1 week	5 days
Philippine Islands	less than 12 hrs – 70 days	12.45 days
Guam	1 day – 16 weeks	27 days
Wake Island	31 days – 12 weeks	49 days

Source: Sample Survey

the refugee becomes an immigrant to a specific country. This state of mind could be said to characterize the transit situation as well as the camp for the Vietnamese refugees, but especially the transit situation. In the interim staging area a decision had to be made whether (1) to immigrate to the United States and accept sponsorship out of the camp, (2) to go to another country, or (3) to return to Vietnam. Some Vietnamese refugees elected the latter two options. This was a decision point for all, even if they merely reaffirmed their choice to come to the United States. Some let themselves drift in this direction of least resistance. Further movements of refugees as well as initial flight often are a direct outcome of the forces acting upon them.

In the case of these Vietnamese, all who wanted to remain in the United States were permitted to do so. They were not, as originally envisioned by some opponents of the Vietnamese refugee resettlement, encouraged or forced to move on to third countries. In this case, trajectory was simpler. One could go to and remain in the United States. The Pacific staging area was, however, "midway to nowhere" in the sense that at that point there were three options (1) the United States, (2) another country, or (3) return to Vietnam. This crisis in decision-making could be agonizing.

Table 40

DAYS TO TRAVEL FROM VIETNAM TO CAMP PENDLETON

Days	Frequency	Percentage
6–10	11	18.6
11–15	2	3.4
16–20	0	
21–25	1	1.7
26–30	6	10.2
31–35	6	10.2
36–40	2	3.4
41–45	2	3.4
46–50	1	1.7
51–55	3	5.1
56–60	3	5.1
61–65	3	5.1
66–70	2	3.4
71–75	2	3.4
76–80		
81–85		
86–90	3	5.1
91–95	3	5.1
96–100		
101–105	1	1.7
105–110	3	5.1
111–115	3	5.1
116–120	1	1.7
121–125	1	1.7
Total	59	100.0

X days for travel was 50.32 days

Source: Sample Survey

Table 41

NUMBER OF STOPS BETWEEN PERMANENT HOME AND CAMP PENDLETON

Number of Stops	Frequency	Percentage
1	1	1.7
2	0	
3	12	20.3
4	24	40.7
5	15	25.4
6	4	6.8
7	3	5.1
Total	59	100.0

Source: Sample Survey

Table 42

ARRIVAL DATE AT PENDLETON

	Frequency	Percentage
During May	12	20.3
During June	22	37.3
During July	18	30.5
During August	6	10.2
During September	1	1.7

Source: Sample Survey

Table 43

WHEN DID YOU FIND OUT WHERE YOU WERE GOING:

Location	Yes	Percentage	Cumulative Percentage
Vietnam	16	27.1	27.1
Guam	10	16.9	44.0
Philippines	11	18.6	62.6
Singapore	2	3.4	66.0
Wake	4	6.8	72.8
Camp Pendleton	3	5.1	77.9
Still Do Not Know	13	22.1	100.0
Total	59	100.0	100.0

Source: Sample Survey

Consider the refugees who did leave the main trajectory at this point. From a report of a mental health team from the National Institute of Mental Health headed by Julius Segal and Norman Lourie who visited the transit camps on Guam:

"Ruminations about the decision to leave Vietnam and about the potential options of returning appeared to weigh heavily in the hearts and minds of the refugees, and pose a mental health issue that is likely to increase in scope and intensity over time. For many refugees—for example, the very old, those with strong and emotional family ties in Vietnam, those without either marketable skills or a knowledge of English, and those for whom departure from Vietnam was sudden, not thoroughly calculated—adaptation to a new life will be slow and tenuous. For such persons, the possibility of returning to Vietnam may increasingly appear attractive as a means for overcoming their chronic crisis of adaptation."—Segal and Lourie, 1975:7-8

Kunz refers to three types of actions, the first and most common being "push-pressure-plunge." After a *push* from the home country, *pressure* follows: ". . . and harassed by the country of asylum and government agencies, the refugee is usually unable to withstand the pressure, and his final acceptance of an offer of settlement is more the taking of a *plunge* than an enthusiastic reaction to a pull." (Kunz, 1973, p. 134) Other alternatives are "push-pressure-stay" and "push-pressure-return."

Repatriation.—In keeping with the United States principle of freedom of movement, and anticipating the possibility that a number of Indochina refugees would want to be repatriated, the Task Force turned to the United Nations High Commission for Refugees (UNHCR) to mediate. Over two thousand refugees, beginning with a group of Vietnamese Air Force personnel, desired to return to their native country. The United States agreed to provide two million dollars to the UNHCR for its expenses and travel costs if the return was accepted by Vietnamese and Cambodian authorities. Little headway was made by UNHCR or the United States over a period of time. By August, the situation at Camp Asan on Guam where the proposed repatriates were quartered was volatile. Despite official difficulties, radio communications were made by the Vietnamese government welcoming the refugees back. The refugees had not been permitted to contact the new government themselves by phone or cable or emissary.

Contacts were limited to diplomatic communiques by the authorities. (Mineta, 1975, p. 9)

On August 19, the refugees on Guam presented a petition requesting use of a Vietnamese ship on Guam to sail back to Vietnam. They pointed out that most of the petitioners had been separated from wives, children, parents, or other family members who remained in Vietnam and that many had left involuntarily. There was a period of increasing tension in the refugee camp—some demonstrations, some violence, and continuing demands for a ship. Following the September 19 visit of the UN High Commission to Vietnam, the report was that there would be no quick response to the request for repatriation. Finally, on September 30, supervised by the Task Force which provided the funds, the U.S. Navy repaired and provisioned the freighter Thuong Tin I and the refugees were advised it would be turned over to them to sail back to Vietnam under the proviso that the United States would assume no responsibility for their safety at sea or their reception in Vietnam. The ship sailed on October 16, with 1,546 repatriates. They all were given final interviews to ascertain their freedom of choice in this matter.

The UNHCR informed the Task Force and State Department on October 31, that the ship had arrived in Vietnam and been accepted. Those refugees were informed that when approval was given by Vietnam and Cambodia they would be repatriated, even if they had been sponsored out of camps in the meantime.

Refugees in and from third countries.—In addition to the repatriates, there were some Vietnamese and Cambodian refugees who preferred third country resettlement and were permitted this option. Data on number of refugees resettled in third countries (total 6,588) is available in the Report to the Congress by the Interagency Task Force (1975b Annex p. 16). The countries drawing substantial numbers of refugees were Canada, 3,926; France 1,836; Australia, 158; Philippines, 114 and Taiwan, 120.

Some refugees who fled to third countries and were in camps there requested to come to the United States. An estimated 12,000 to 15,000 Vietnamese, Cambodians, and Laotians were in refugee camps in Malaysia, Hong Kong, Thailand, and Korea. Of these, approximately 6,000 had relatives in the United States

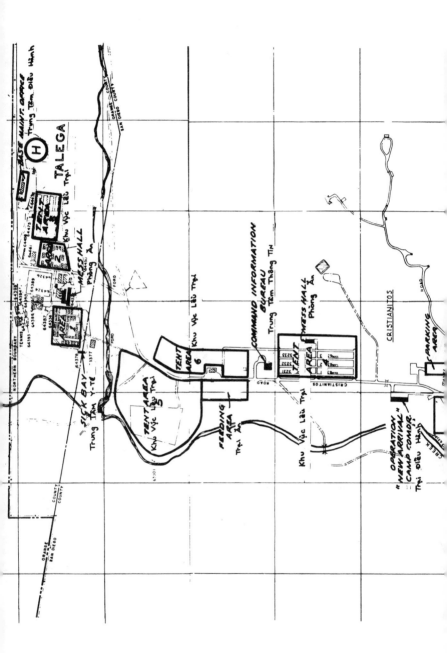

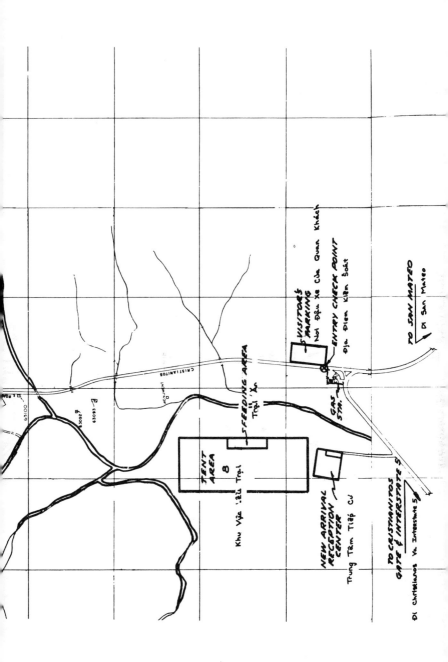

and, therefore, were eligible for parole. In addition, 40,000 Meo tribesmen, many of whom worked for the CIA, escaped from Laos into Thailand and are situated on Thai military bases.

The Task Force negotiated with the foreign governments to seek release of those refugees who had relatives in the United States. The process was slow, and in at least one hundred cases the Vietnamese had to wait several months before being transported to rejoin their relatives in the United States.

Concern also was expressed about conditions in the third country refugee camps, thought to be "unsafe, unsanitary, and unlivable." Refugees in the camps were observed to have signs of malnutrition and illness. (Mineta, *et.al.*, 1975, pp. 6-7)

As of the December 15 report of the Interagency Task Force (IATF, 1975b), about 80,000 Indo-Chinese refugees still were stranded in Thailand and in a number of other countries in Southeast Asia. The State Department agreed, with cooperation of the Immigration and Naturalization Service, to parole additional refugees on a selective basis, especially from Thailand whose regular quotas had been exhausted by the number of eligible refugees. Some consideration was given to admitting additional refugees up to the ceiling of 150,000 using already appropriated funds (IATF, Report to the Congress 1975b, p. 18). Apparently the extension of parole to the refugees beyond the numerical and financial limits previously decided upon was not considered. Even though some of the refugees remaining in third countries were closely associated with the United States or the fallen Indochinese governments, they were not in a position to settle permanently in their current countries of residence. They were expected to be admitted to the United States and processed by traditional resettlement channels, not the Task Force refugee processing (IATF, 1975b, p. 19). The effective exclusion of these refugees from the United States illustrates the limitations on entry into refugee status maintained by the United States. Refugee parole (refugee status) was *not* extended to its logical limits to include these refugees, in spite of their affiliation with the United States, simply because by chance they escaped and ended up in third countries.

An additional group of 127 refugees were third country nationals evacuated from Vietnam, citizens of the Philippines, Korea, and Taiwan, who remained on Guam after the close of the camp until December 31, and were permitted to find jobs if they could. Their ultimate designation is not certain.

The psychology of "Midway to Nowhere."—In addition to the main trajectory from Vietnam to Pacific staging base to the United States camp there were some refugees who (1) went on to third countries, (2) went first to third countries before coming to the United States; (3) some refugees still remaining in third countries; and (4) some citizens of other countries remaining as refugees on Guam. These categories of persons illustrate the complex kinetics of the refugee movements, comprising not only the initial "push" with which the refugee almost involuntarily exits his country but extending also to his subsequent movements.

"Kinetics, *the branch of dynamics which investigates the relations between the motions of bodies and the forces acting upon them," has been preferred to the more general term* dynamics, *which when used in social sciences suggests the existence of an inner self-propelling force. In the writer's view this inner force is singularly absent from the movement of refugees. Their progress more often than not resembles the movement of the billiard ball: devoid of inner direction their path is governed by the kinetic factors of inertia, friction and the vectors of outside forces applied on them."*—Kunz, 1975:131

Thinking of this model from the inside out, that is in terms of the social psychology of the process of becoming a refugee, surely there must be some psychological stress in being the "billiard ball," reminiscent of Laing's psychiatric patient described as a tennis ball volleyed by the forces of her family. (Laing, 1969, pp. 15-17). In terms of locus of control (Rotter, 1966) or attribution of cause and effectiveness (Heider, 1958, Thibant and Riecken, 1955), the refugees felt the mastery and control over their own fate must be very low, with concomitant effects on adjustment and mental health.

In addition to the lack of initiative and helplessness, *vis-a-vis* one's destiny present in the refugees in the midway-to-nowhere predicament, a sharp loss of the usual social supports had just been experienced. The refugee, from a society which supports and values long-term personal ties, experienced a sharp severance of the social fabric of family, friends, neighborhood, and work groups into which he had been integrated. He experienced the trauma of separation from these social networks and the loss of their support in this crisis.

Two consultants from the National Institute of Mental Health, Segal and Lourie, visited a number of installations on Guam and conducted intensive interviews with thirty refugees and families in addition to a second round of shorter interviews. They commented: *"Especially considering the stressful nature of their current existence, the Vietnamese refugees are remarkably disciplined and cooperative in their behavior; surprisingly little evidence of delinquency or other anti-social behavior is apparent."*—Segal and Lourie, 1975:5)

However, they also expressed concern that: *"Although the number of psychiatric casualties treated to date has been insignificant (seven cases), this cannot be viewed as a barometer of overall psychological distress among the refugee population; the stresses which brought only a handful of patients to treatment exist in abundance in the larger population. Furthermore, it is likely that mental health problems, including serious emotional breakdowns, will increase over time as the ambiguities of life outside Vietnam and the shock of family separation increase, and coping and adaptation resources are stretched beyond reasonable limits.*

"Natural tendencies toward fearfulness, docility, and the masking of feeling, especially in their current predicament, serve to hide the considerable array of potentially overwhelming emotional problems which exist among the Vietnamese refugees. Prominent among these are feelings of grief and depression, anxiety about the welfare of separated family members, panic over an uncertain future, feelings of remorse and guilt, confusion, and a growing sense of bitterness, disappointment and anger. The emotional burdens carried by the refugees are often detected not only in a general sense of malaise, fatigue, and psychosomatic complaints, but by evidence of lethargy, withdrawal and seclusion, huddling, expressions of melancholy, and crying in private."—Segal and Lourie, 1975:4

American caretaking effort.—The response of the host country to the refugee exodus in terms of assistance in the transit was heroic, as noted by Segal and Lourie (1975, p. 1), but left a gap *vis-a-vis* needs and expectations. Response in terms of psychological needs was particularly insufficient. Effort was directed toward material provisions but not "spiritual" nourishment.

Like the evacuation, the transit phase of the refugee process was the responsibility of the military services, who on extremely short notice, had to select and establish a number of Pacific staging areas. Responsibility for logistics, including transportation, was given to the Defense Department and military service. Administration of staging areas included military and civilian coordinators.

Congressman Mineta's fact-finding report states that "there have been no negative reports concerning the Pacific reception sites that process refugees en route to the U.S." (Mineta *et. al.* 1975, p. 8) except for the aforementioned Camp Asan on Guam where 1,804 of the 2,338 refugees were awaiting repatriation.

Problems noted by Segal and Lourie were those of the discrepant time dimension—perspectives of the refugees as compared with their caretakers.

"The mental health problems of the refugees on Guam reflect themes that merge their life experiences prior to their departure, their present life on Guam, and their anticipations of their destinies upon arrival in mainland camps. The essential demands of caring for and processing the refugee population on Guam often tends to focus attention on their current experience as a discrete and unconnected episode, removed from what went before and what is to follow ni the lives of these people. The result is an increase in the refugee's sense of isolation and abandonment and the potential for serious mental health problems."—Segal and Lourie, 1975:6

While an heroic logistic effort has been noted:

"Logistical and administrative concerns merge with emotional and psychological ones at the day-to-day operating level in such matters as out-processing, feeding, transportation, and other basic elements of camp life. In the absence of appropriate training and supervision or of special selection procedures, the skills and experience of the enlisted staff who deal with refugees in these and similar contexts are not always equal to the task of providing warm, accepting, and constructive interactions that are likely to improve rather than diminish the refugee's mental health.

"However subtly expressed, signs of hostility and lack of empathy among those relating to the refugees–including those in the

surrounding population–carry with them harmful effects on the potential for a satisfactory adaptation in the United States.

"Insufficient attention to the habits and customs of the Vietnamese cultures creates among many refugees a sense of isolation and rejection. The result is an increased vulnerability to depression and a poor transition to the new environment."— Segal and Lourie, 1975:6-7

The consultants went on to recommend special counseling services and sensitizing (training programs) to be undertaken with staff. Recommendation also was made for utilization of a "person expert in the Vietnamese culture" or "qualified and already well-integrated refugees" in dealing with a continuing issue (of adjustment) to be discussed at great length in connection with the mainland camps.

Finally, the problem of continuity of concern was evident, i.e., 1) liaison and mutual exchange of information between Guam and other Pacific sites and stateside camps; 2) reduction of repeated moves from one camp to another on Guam; and 3) disruption of extended families, transience, cultural shock, and loss. These were regarded mostly as an inevitable concomitant of the refugee experience and as the perhaps necessary tendency to concentrate on physical tasks and processing without much empathy for the disjointed and negative experiences of the refugees. As Segal and Lourie put it:

*"It is recognized that the circumstances of the Vietnamese refugee operation precluded the rapid institution of many of the programs of action recommended here. Current procedures reflect an absence of options rather than a lack of sensitivity and concern for human welfare."—*Segal and Lourie, 1975:11

Of course, almost by definition and except for repatriates and third country refugees, the transit was a temporary experience, again marked by different perspectives and concerns of refugees and host with the refugees being quite uncomfortable in an alien culture and preoccupied by losses and fears; the host concentrating upon physical survival and immediate material needs. The gap in the interchange was quite evident.

As of September 4, 1975, there were 2,338 refugees on Guam, 1,802 awaiting repatriation, while the other centers were closed in June (Clark Air Force Base), July (Wake Island), and August (Subic Bay). Hickam Field retained nine refugees as of September 4, 1975 (Mineta *et. al.*, 1975, p. 8).

5
At Camp Pendleton

The means by which help is being mechanically provided are (very) numerous, yet the receiving end cannot still be satisfied due to different concepts and needs.—A refugee

We can best begin discussion of the camp phase of the refugee process from the point of view of the agents of the host country. The host had the initiative in choosing and providing facilities, the reception centers or "camps," while the refugees adjusted and responded to these efforts.

The refugee camp and its provision of services.—Camp Pendleton in southern California, the first refugee camp, opened with the expectation of accommodating 18,000 refugees; Fort Chaffee in Arkansas opened in early May to receive some 24,000 refugees; and Eglin Air Force Base in Florida opened on May 4 to receive 5,000 refugees; Indiantown Gap in Pennsylvania was the last camp opened.

On April 29, Brigadier General Graham, Commanding General of Camp Pendleton, received a phone call announcing that within twenty-four hours preparation must be made to receive nearly 20,000 refugees from Indo-China. Instant preparations were made to house, clothe, and feed a population of that size. Marine Corps personnel worked around the clock to establish eight separate tent areas; plumbing was installed to bring water supply to the tented areas, a normal security system was installed, and the stockpile of food was prepared for 20,000 refugees. Large numbers of refugees arrived in the middle of the night beginning in May. They were met on the beaches by emergency workers from the camp, to be processed and transported to the tent areas.

Arrival on the beaches in southern California in the middle of the night represented the final step of a long, fearful and anxiety-ridden journey characterized by frequent translocation and the uncertainty of a final destination. For the overwhelming majority of the refugees, the journey was at least three weeks long; and for many, the journey was more than two months in duration. In this sudden change of life situation, accompanied in many cases by a drastic disruption of kinship or family relations and the loss of loved ones; amidst a confused and ambiguous situation as to what-has-happened and what-will-happen, the refugees were greeted by the coldest spring in years for southern California and were supplied upon their arrival with nothing but a government-issued flight jacket.

The Marine Corps report "Operation New Arrivals" (U.S.M.C., 1975), describes the organization, services, and facilities provided the refugees by the Marines at Camp Pendleton. The report describes the three phases of camp growth as 1) rapid increase in camp population and initial establishment of the camp to provide essential services (April 26 to May 12); 2) a more permanent establishment of the camp, elaboration of services, and stabilization of camp population (May 13 to August 31); and 3) a phasing out of services and facilities as the population declined (Sept. 1 to Oct. 21).

Each camp unit was to provide its population with housing, food, and showers; facilities for washing, sanitation, recreation, and education; child care, children's playgrounds, and limited medical assistance. (See pp. 12-14, U.S.M.C., 1975 for more detail.) Essentially, a tent camp facility for over 20,000 refugees was established in less than twenty-four hours.

A number of federal agencies contributed their services to the refugees and these contributions are detailed in "Information About the Indochina Refugee Resettlement Program" (U.S. Dept. of H.E.W., 1975). The Department of Defense was responsible for military coordination, logistics and facilities, Interagency Task Force, civilians (mostly employees of AID), State Department, USIA, and HEW for civilian coordination with responsibility for administration. The State Department's contribution to the Task Force was funding and administration as well as handling refugees in third countries. The Office of Management and Budget helped with budgeting, and financial contributions; the Department of Labor with job skill evaluation, job matching, and labor supply information; the Immigration and Naturalization Service of the Justice Department with clearance and processing, and the Justice Department supplied U.S. Marshalls for security for the repatriates and an attorney from the Attorney General's Office; the USIA helped with preparation of materials; GSA with supervision; the Small Business Department ran seminars; the Department of Transportation arranged travel; the Treasury Department organized financial exchange opportunities, and HUD provided information on federally assisted housing programs. ("After Action Report," U.S.M.C., 1975 and Mineta *et. al.*, 1975 contain further information about specific services and programs.) Other activities in the Camp included: registration with Immigration and Naturalization Service and HEW, Public Health Screening, and registration with VOLAG (voluntary agencies) for sponsorship.

On May 12 at the end of Phase One, the population of the Camp stood at 18,566. During Phase Two an additional 23,265 more Vietnamese and Cambodians came to Camp Pendleton from Pacific staging areas, with approximately 210 arriving each day. In the final phase 29,135 departed the Camp, averaging 262 per day.

"These statistics . . . provide some indication of the dynamic situation which continued to prevail, requiring a 24-hour day operation and creating constant administrative and logistic problems of major proportions."—USMC, 1975:31

As the camp moved into a more stabilized period, services proliferated and the camp became more of a temporary home rather than a facility for transients. Such services included: post exchange privileges, opportunity to sell gold, bank services, cafeteria, recreation (sports, entertainment including TV, movies, bingo, dancing, talent shows), some day care (1,000 children in each of the six main camps), libraries, sewing centers, education (from survival English to university level in seventy-two tents with one hundred teachers per day and 70 percent of the refugee population active in the program at any one time), improved sanitation, communication—telephone, telegraph, and radio message service, camp newspaper in Vietnamese, English, Cambodian and Chinese—some Vietnamese food, ten religious programs, especially Roman Catholic and Buddhist, (as well as

Protestant clergymen, organized by the refugee population, augmented by monks from a local Buddhist temple hired by the chaplain's office). Over eighty weddings were performed in camp during the five month period.

"Religion played an important role in the lives of the refugees and all religious activities were well attended."—U.S.M.C., 19-75:39

Refugee life in Camp Pendleton.—A refugee infrastructure was set up consisting of a refugee coordinator down to a senior officer in charge of each hut or tent. This expedited communication with refugees, sanitation, policing, education, recreation, medical services, supply records, and maintenance of tents. On the other hand, the final report of the camp's commander suggested limitations in the use of refugees as manpower because of the language barrier, the time spent in processing and classes, family responsibilities, transience, and resentment of the authority by other refugees (as well as the tendency of such refugees to use their assignment for personal gain). (U.S.M.C., 1975, pp. 48-49)

The majority (58.7 percent) of the refugees did not know if there were leaders they could go to for help. (See Table 44.) Another fifty-five (27.4 percent) stated there was no leadership in Camp Pendleton. Only twenty-seven or 13.4 percent of the refugees knew who to look to for leadership and they gave thirty-four names of leaders. The positions these leaders possessed in Vietnam are shown in Table 45. Military officers of the Vietnamese army serving as heads of the camp and priests most often were seen as the leaders of the camp. Others viewed as leaders were doctors, parents, teachers, lawyers, Vietnamese colleagues, and Vietnamese married to Americans.

Reasons for selecting leaders were, "He is the leader among us because he teaches us the good and knows the bad things to avoid." "He is strict, systematic, and knows how to handle people."

Sixty-three percent of the refugees claimed they didn't know them, they didn't trust them, or they didn't need them when questioned about the lack of Vietnamese leadership. (See Table 46.) They rejected fellow countrymen as capable of helping them out of their present situation.

The refugees found everything in a state of confusion in their

Table 44

REFUGEES' PERCEPTIONS ON LEADERSHIP IN THE CAMP

	Frequency	Percentage
Yes	27	13.4
It Depends	1	.5
No	55	27.4
Don't Know	11.8	58.7
No Answer	1	----
Total	202	100.0

Table 45

REFUGEES' PERCEPTIONS AS TO WHO WERE THE LEADERS

Positions	Frequency	Percentage
Priest	8	22.1
Head of Camp	2	5.3
Vietnam Officers	8	21.1
Doctors	3	7.8
Parents	2	5.3
Others	8	21.1
Don't Know	4	10.5
Other Professionals	3	7.8
Total	38	100.0

Table 46

REFUGEES' PERCEPTIONS AS TO WHY HAVE LEADERS NOT EMERGED

	Frequency	Percentage
Lack of Dedication	3	5.1
Lack of Ability	4	6.8
Corruption	3	5.1
Everyone is Equal	2	3.4
Don't Know Them	17	28.8
Don't Trust Them	14	23.7
Don't Need Them	6	10.1
Other Reasons	8	13.6
Don't Know	2	3.4
Total	59	100.0

evacuation. They had lost trust in the Vietnamese leadership. Therefore, overwhelming numbers of refugees refused to acknowledge leaders. Many stated they, "Lost all confidence in Thieu and Minh and their leaders." Other statements were, "No trust in those who led us before." "Can't find because of past experience." "Do not trust anyone anymore." The refugees were very cautious in trusting again. Their past experiences showed them that their leaders were unworthy. Their statements reflect their opinion of the Vietnamese leadership: "Most Vietnamese coming here are part of a corrupted social system." "Most Vietnamese are greedy and corrupt." "Vietnamese leaders lack dedication, capability, and are too corrupt." "There are lots of able persons but they only want to help themselves and their families. Lots of people want to take advantage of the refugees just like they took advantage of the Vietnamese in Vietnam then." Even the clergy were not immune from suspicions of the refugees. One Vietnamese stated: "Before we put all belief in the clergy, now we know there are those who are good and also those who are not. We have lost all trust in the Vietnamese people. We must silently bear them."

To be leaders they had to prove they were worthy. Among the reasons given by the refugees for the lack of leadership in Camp Pendleton was that they were not qualified. Some statements reflecting this kind of thought are: "Those whom I know do not have the capabilities." "No one so far has displayed enough qualifications to be the ldeader." "They work with no pay, so do not work conscientiously for everybody." Some claimed they had tried, but were unable, to find any leaders. They were seeking leaders who could understand the "personal lives" of the refugees.

Some of the refugees were very unsure of their own ability to judge who would make a good leader. One Vietnamese said, "I do not have enough intelligence to know who is a good or bad leader." Another says "do not trust anyone." "All leaders in camp are strangers to me, so do not know their characters. Do not know whether they can be leaders or not."

When a problem arose, the refugees looked to their own families for support. It was quite common for them to feel "No one is trustworthy other than direct family members." Similar feelings are reflected in these statements, "Do not rely on anyone totally but my own family." "Do not know and do not trust anyone but family." Some felt they could only depend on themselves in an emergency. "I do not think I could find any leaders. Anytime I want to do something, just do it myself."

Ten percent of the group vowed they had no need for any leaders. "Everybody is equal and on the same level." "Only need spiritual leadership, no other kinds." Some stated the reason they did not need any leaders was because they had not met any difficulties requiring outside help.

Many refugees withdrew from contact with other Vietnamese. A typical kind of statement was, "Spent most of the time in the tent, not much contact with others, so do not know well their qualifications." Many had little or no contact with others. They refused to have anything to do with fellow Vietnamese. This does not in any way mean that there was a lack of leadership in Camp Pendleton but a lack of desire on the part of the refugees to recognize anybody as leaders.

From the perspective of the social structure in the camp, it was quite obvious that refugees arrived at different times from quite divergent routes and were a heterogeneous population. Although they were interviewed within the first ninety days of their arrival, many were interviewed only a few days after their arrival. It is logical to assume that leadership eventually would have emerged had it not been for the transitory nature of the camp. As the social situation and routines of life became more stable there would have been the emergence of leadership. What was significant, though perhaps not surprising, is the fact that no former office holders were recognized as leaders. Mr. Ky, the former Vice President of the South Vietnamese government, a resident in Camp 8, was not identified as a leader in spite of the fact that he was sought after by media reporters.

There were no severe health or discipline problems at Camp Pendleton, according to the Marine Corps report. In spite of the lack of privacy, close living conditions, and inadequate means to safeguard valuables, thievery was relatively uncommon. The most frequent discipline incidents were interpersonal altercations among family members or neighbors, usually resolved informally by the military camp commander and the Vietnamese coordinator.

To locate a specific refugee was difficult, according to the

USMC report, because of the language barrier and the propensity to move to be with relatives or friends or to be in better facilities. Refugees tended to sort themselves out into groups representing Vietnamese social strata—peasants, middle-class, single army officers, etc.

Daily routines in the camp.—After the uncertainties en route to the camp, the deadly enemy for the refugees during the long hours of waiting was the lack of meaningful and organized activities. People spent hours standing in queues for food. Members of the family had to take turns to eat in order to watch whatever belongings they had with them in the tent. Children could be seen playing around those tents but adults were told they must stay close to their tent areas in case they were needed by the Camp Commander or by sponsors. Volunteers organized English language classes. The longer the wait for sponsorship, the more bored the refugee felt. On the other hand, the more bored, the longer the wait seems. In Camp Pendleton, unlike other camps, no refugee was asked to help at meal time or to prepare food.

Table 47

AVERAGE CAMP DAY ACTIVITIES

	Frequency	Percent of 59
Stand in Chow Line	37	62.7
Visit Friends	10	16.9
Take Care of Children	3	5.1
Reading	7	11.9
Leisure Activities	18	30.5
Sports Exercise	6	10.2
Study English	13	22.0
Go to Classes	14	23.7
Work Job	4	6.8
Sponsor Prospects	2	3.4
Laundry	16	27.1
Bath	5	8.5
Household Work	3	5.1
Orientation	3	5.1
Others	11	18.6

The most often cited daily activity was to wait for chow. Sixty-three percent or thirty-seven heads of households averaged 2 hours 15 minutes daily dining including the time they stood in line for their meals. Other daily routine activities commonly done were laundry (27.1 percent), bathing (8.5 percent), taking care of the children (5.1 percent) and household work (5.1 percent).

There were twenty-seven heads of households or 55.7 percent who spent time attending classes or studying English an average of four hours daily. This was felt to be the most necessary requirement if they were to function outside of camp and acquire jobs. They wanted to overcome their language deficiency.

Living in a camp which provided for everything obviously gave the refugees a lot of free time. In fact, they probably had too much of it. One respondent said he was not used to doing nothing.

Leisure time activities included various activities such as reading newspapers and magazines, watching television, playing music, sewing and knitting. Eighteen heads of households spent an average of 3.35 hours pursuing the above activities. Ten Vietnamese heads of households or 16.9 percent visited friends for about an average of three and a half hours daily. Walking was the daily exercise for 10.2 percent and another 10.2 percent pursued some sports activities.

Table 48

AVERAGE CAMP DAY

	Frequency	Percent of 59
Stand in Chow Line	37	62.7
Visit Friends	10	16.9
Take Care of Children	3	5.1
Reading	7	11.9
Leisure Activities	18	30.5
Sports Exercise	6	10.2
Study English	13	22.0
Go to Classes	14	23.7
Work, Job	4	6.8
Sponsor Prospects	2	3.4
Laundry	16	27.1
Bath	5	8.5
Household Work	3	5.1
Orientation	3	5.1
Others	11	18.5

Description of Camp Pendleton by a visiting journalist can add to our impression of camp life. (We must recall again that in discussing Camp Pendleton there is no information on other camps based on systematic study.) Chuman of the Japanese Los Angeles Daily paper visited Pendleton in late May, about the beginning of the stable phase. He likened the setting of the Camp to a set for M.A.S.H., noting the refugees much preferred tents to quonset huts because the sheet metal heated rapidly in the daytime but retained cold at night.

Table 49

ACTIVITY DURING AVERAGE DAY

Activity	Number of Participants	Mean Amt. of Time Spent
Eating Chow	37	2 hr 15 min
Attend Class, School		
Study English	27	4 hr
Teach English	2	2 hr
Laundry	16	45 min
Bath	5	54 min
Work	5	6.6 hr
Visit Friends	10	3.38 hr
Reads News & Mag.	8	2 hr
Play Music	5	4.2 hr
Walk	8	1.5 hr
Sports	6	1.67 hr

"As you walk or drive through the refugee camps, one phenomenon noticed after awhile is the constant movement within the camps. This is especially true in the Vietnamese camps. If the refugees are out of their tents or quonsets, they are on the move. Whether they are going anywhere is debatable, but clusters of young refugees were continuously moving in groups of four or more. While smaller children scurried about at play, the older refugees just walked to mess halls, to the latrines, to the medical dispensary, to mobile post exchanges, to other camps to search for relatives or friends—the strolling seemed endless and the constant patternless flux of this tide of humanity was lulling, nearly hypnotic to watch."—Chuman, RAFU Shimpo, May 21, 1975

Chuman heard some complaints about the food and noted that many of the refugees were accustomed to military food as employees of the U.S. or South Vietnamese armies. On the other hand, Chuman found ridiculous the Marine Corps claim that the food had been adjusted to Vietnamese taste. With the exception of steamed rice, he found this not to be true. Chuman also found the Vietnamese newspaper was a mimeo bulletin which did not report Vietnamese news as adequately as the *Los Angeles Times*.

Chuman attempted to debunk a popular view that these Vietnamese escapees were rich profiteers. He found them to be basically middle class. He also found they gave little serious consideration to returning to South Vietnam, contrary to some popular impressions of the time.

"One refugee . . . said that although he is not having a good time at Camp Pendleton, he has no choice but to stay."—Chuman, Rafu Shimpo, May 22, 1975

"A woman said, 'If I know life in the United States would be like this maybe I would not come here, but I have nothing left in my country now either.'"—Chuman, Rafu Shimpo, May 22, 1975

Data from the Asian American Mental Health Research Center's Camp Pendleton survey, however, provides a less positive view of Vietnamese attitude toward life in camp. When asked "Considering this is not a real home but only a temporary place to stay, what things, if any, do you like most about this camp?" Thirty-three of the fifty-nine heads of households responded they found *nothing* about the camp they liked.

Table 50

WHAT DO YOU LIKE ABOUT CAMP PENDLETON:

	Frequency	Percentage
American Generosity	8	22.2
American Attitude	5	13.9
Camp Food	4	11.1
Camp Lodging	2	5.6
Presence of Vietnamese	4	11.1
Other Reasons	13	36.1
Total	36	100.0

One Vietnamese responded, "Since this is only a temporary shelter, we can accept and endure any hardships. No complaints." Another Vietnamese stated, "I do not like anything, on the contrary, very depressed in this camp." The other twenty-six respondents gave thirty-six reasons why they liked Camp Pendleton. This is shown in Table 50.

American generosity was appreciated by eight respondents. They liked the help they received from the Americans. Appreciative statements included, "Very touched by the way the Americans have lent their help." "Help has been given in every aspect—health, sanitation, food, and entertainment." "I like the way Americans work to help us. When I lost something, the processing center called and gave it back to me. No kleptomaniacs."

Five Vietnamese commented on the kindness and good treatment they received from the Americans. The following statements are in the Vietnamese' own words: "I like the freedom and openness of many Americans." "We are well treated by the U.S. servicemen. There is politeness and respect for all religious beliefs." "I like the way the U.S. marines treat me." "The U.S. government has been very kind as far as food and lodging are concerned."

Six Vietnamese heads of households reported they liked not having to "worry or be concerned about life-sustaining needs." Three statements supporting this idea were: "Have enough food and decent chow hall." "Good and careful setup of food and lodging." "No cooking to do."

The presence of other Vietnamese was another reason given for liking Camp Pendleton. Examples of this kind of response were "Like living together with many other Vietnamese." "I like seeing again other Vietnamese and making new friends." "Nothing special to like except like the presence of many Vietnamese around."

Other reasons the Vietnamese liked Camp Pendleton were the "education programs for the children," and "ability to attend English classes."

One must allow the possibility that this failure of the Vietnamese interviewees to cite positive features of the camp does not necessarily reflect an inadequacy of camp facilities but partially, at least, may reflect the state of mind of the refugees and the relative deprivation experienced *vis-a-vis* their circumstances and lifestyle in Vietnam.

The Vietnamese seemed to adjust to camp well. To the question, "During the past week in this camp, did you have the feeling that anyone in your family or someone else living with you had a disturbing problem?" the majority or 78.1 percent of the respondents replied no. Only forty-three individuals or 21.4 percent were aware that people living with them had problems. It can be assumed that in spite of the difficult situation at Camp Pendleton, the refugees were adjusting. The heads of households, non-relatives residing with the family, and mothers of the heads of households most frequently suffered the problems. (See Table 51.)

Trouble with sponsors was the most frequently cited cause of problems in camp. The heads of households were the most troubled members of the family because they had the responsibility for the family's future. Where could the family go after Camp Pendleton? They had to find a good sponsor.

At the time of the interview (between August and September, 1977), the majority or 64.4 percent of the heads of households had no sponsorship prospects. Of the 33.9 percent who had sponsorship possibilities, 25.4 percent had contacts with their sponsors but 11.9 percent still had not.

Stress caused by troubles with sponsors included confusion in paperwork, rejection, loss of patience waiting to hear from a sponsor, difference of opinion from sponsor, as well as no sponsor. Confusion with papers included the "loss of the entire family files," and "mix-up in paperwork which is causing delays in exit." Those who faced rejection by a sponsor were quite bitter. One such refugee stated, "I was promised to be sponsored and now the application is rejected by the sponsor. I am very critical of this system and hate Americans." High hopes when dashed were so disappointing for the refugees.

Refugees waited daily to hear from their sponsors. Bored and tired, their anxiety levels rose and their patience grew thin. One entire family was processed to leave camp, and then for eight days waited for the agency-promised airplane tickets to Ohio.

Some refugees had differences of opinions with their sponsors. "Everyone in our family had troubles with the sponsor who wants us to live in the countryside. We want to go to a city." Another Vietnamese felt his problem was that he had no freedom in camp. He wanted to stay in California but the sponsor was in Missouri.

Domestic problems between family members were common in

Table 51

DID A FAMILY MEMBER OR SOMEONE ELSE LIVING WITH YOU
HAVE A DISTURBING PROBLEM DURING THE PAST WEEK?

	Frequency	Percentage
Yes	43	21.4
No	157	78.1
Total	200	99.5

Table 52

RELATIONSHIP OF THE PERSON WITH THE PROBLEM

	Frequency	Percentage
Head of Household	10	18.2
Spouse	1	1.8
Son	4	7.3
Daughter	1	1.8
Father of HH	4	7.3
Mother of HH	6	10.9
Spouse Father	2	3.6
Brother of HH	2	3.6
Sister of HH	2	3.6
Aunt of HH	2	3.6
Uncle of HH	1	1.8
Grandchild of HH	1	1.8
Non-Relatives	10	18.2
Other Relatives	3	5.6
Other	6	10.9
Total	55	100.0

Table 53

CAUSES OF THE PROBLEM

Problem	Frequency	Percentage
Domestic	11	20.8
Argument	4	7.6
Lost Relatives	5	9.4
Lost Fortune	2	3.8
Sick or Accident	7	13.2
Camp Conditions	7	13.2
Trouble Re: Sponsor	12	22.6
Others	5	9.4
Total	53	100.0

Camp Pendleton. The high anxiety states created by the traumatic evacuation and future uncertainty combined with many family members crowded in small living quarters, minimum privacy, and too much spare time made arguments surface easily. Mothers argued with their children. Wives screamed at their husbands. Teenagers argued with friends. The disputes often were over "many small things" such as friends deciding how to set up a party. No longer the productive, active breadwinners, fathers had a difficult time gaining the respect of the family. They no longer listened to him and his influence diminished. Fathers felt useless and depressed. Distress weakened the family. Examples of statements showing a difference of opinion with fathers: "My father is too nervous. He always thinks he is right and will not listen to others. In other words, he is too conservative." "My problem is my father always reprimands me. He does not understand and sympathize with me." Some quarrels went too far and some family members wanted to live apart from the family to avoid conflicts. One father stated, "My son wants to live apart once out of camp. He no longer wants to be in the same group with us."

Health problems concerned several refugees. Some were concerned about those who refused to seek medical help. One Vietnamese found it "very disturbing to me that a Chinese national in the same barracks coughs a lot and still will not go to the dispensary." Others felt they did not "get good treatment," or were confused by the doctors, such as this refugee, "I have troubles with medical exams. Some MD's say I am sick and others say I am fine." Other reasons given for seeking medical help were: "My son broke his arm playing soccer." "My sister is sick with water in her leg bone." "My three friends are sick with the flu." One family suffered the death of their grandmother.

Camp Pendleton conditions disliked by the refugees were given in a previous section. They did, however, again voice strong feelings about the food, adding their dislike in having to accept this food. Statements such as "Mother is resentful of the charity of chow," and "Our entire family feels we have to beg for food and live like prisoners," show that they were not accustomed to being dependent on others for their welfare.

Other problems mentioned were not getting mail and the loss of belongings, clothes, and money. The activities of their neighbors were bothersome. When people live in such close proximity they can hear the quarrels next door or the disruptions created by the "man next door with his seven wives."

Relatives left Vietnam with 39.0 percent of the refugee families. (See Table 54.) Another 17.5 percent had relatives join them in Camp Pendleton. There were twelve family members reunited in ten families. (See Table 55.)

Refugees continued to miss family members. A lady missed her husband. Another lost contact with her elder son who tried to find his own way out of Vietnam. A father searched for his younger brother from whom he was separated. These families wanted to be together with all members intact.

Table 54

DID OTHER RELATIVES LEAVE VIETNAM
WITH YOU?

	Frequency	Percentage
Yes	23	39.0
No	33	55.9
No Response	3	5.1
Total	59	100.0

Table 55

WERE OTHER RELATIVES REUNITED IN CAMP PENDLETON?

	Frequency	Percentage
Yes	10	17.5
No	47	82.5
No Response	2	----
Total	59	100.0

From whom would the Vietnamese seek help in Camp Pendleton if they encountered a problem? (See Table 57.) Overwhelming numbers or 32.2 percent of the refugees would ask camp authorities such as the head of the camp, processor, competent authorities, Camp Services or the Red Cross to assist them. Many emphasized the words "competent" and "responsible" in their descriptions of camp helpers. For example "Go directly to

Table 56

WHO ARE THE REUNITED RELATIVES

	Frequency
Brother to HH	1
Uncle of HH	1
Spouse Aunt	1
Cousin of HH	4
Non-Relatives	1
Niece of HH	1
Other Relatives	3
Total	12

Table 57

CAMP HELPER IF NEEDED ASSISTANCE WITH
A PROBLEM

	Frequency	Percentage	
Head of Camp	34	16.8)	
Processor	11	5.4)	
Red Cross	8	4.0)	32.2
Competent Authority	8	4.0)	
Camp Services	4	2.0)	
Parents	10	5.0)	
Spouse	3	1.4)	
Siblings	12	6.0)	17.4
Family in General	10	5.0)	
Friends	6	3.0)	
Priest	11	5.4)	8.4
Doctor	4	2.0)	
Interpreter	2	1.0)	
Have Not Found Anyone Yet	29	14.3)	
Don't Know Them	3	1.5)	25.2
Don't Trust Them	1	.5)	
Don't Need Them	18	8.9)	
Others	15	7.4)	
Don't Know	10	5.0)	
No Answer	3	1.4)	
Total	202		

competent American authorities." "Ask the knowledgeable ones with instructive and helpful ideas." "Those involved who are competent on the matter." The refugees wanted responsible help. They also felt that those with a knowledge of English would be in a better position to assist them. Typical answers were "I can ask whoever can speak English" or "The interpreter because he is fluent in English."

There were 25 percent of this sample who would not seek any help or would do so with great reluctance. Twenty-nine refugees answered "Have not found anyone yet." Some did respond that they "have not needed any help in camp yet." One Vietnamese stated, "I did all work by myself. Besides there is nothing so hard that requires help from anyone." Others who had not faced any problems responded, "We are not very much in need of help." "Have not thought and do not know where or who to turn to for help." "No one has offered any help and we did not look for any help." Some Vietnamese were reluctant to trust anyone again. They made these kind of statements, "No more trust in any one." "Never go to anybody." "Never rely on anyone again." They would solve their problems themselves.

There were 17.4 percent who relied on family members to help them solve their problems. Some families designated a family member to deal with their concerns. For example, "Husband takes care of all problems." "Sister works in the processing center and takes care of everything." "Rely on children to seek information." Friends were a source of assistance for a few Vietnamese. One Vietnamese stated seeking help from "friends who were classmates in Vietnam and along in this exodus." Another stated, "The aged ones who worked with me in Vietnam." Length of friendship was important. If help was given in Vietnam by a military officer or priest, the refugees continued to be grateful and sought these people out for help. They had proven they could be trusted.

Priests, doctors and representative of the refugees were sources of help for 8.4 percent of the sample. Significantly, there is the tendency to identify the person. For example, "Father Linh, the priest; we have known since the exile in 1954 from North Vietnam."

Considering everything, including the failure to note positive features of camp life, complaints were not too great. When asked for "the things you dislike most about this camp" out of fifty-nine heads of households twenty indicated "no complaints." (See Table 58.)

One Vietnamese stated, "I do not dislike anything because only plan on staying here in the camp temporarily." The other 63.6 percent or thirty-nine respondents gave fifty-six reasons for why they disliked camp.

Table 58

WHAT DO YOU DISLIKE ABOUT CAMP PENDLETON?

	Frequency	Percentage
No Response	20	36.4
Responded	39	63.6
Total	59	100.0

Table 59

REASONS GIVEN BY 39 HEADS OF HOUSEHOLDS FOR THEIR DISLIKE OF CAMP PENDLETON

Reasons	Frequency	Percentage
Camp Food	10	17.9
Living Conditions	9	16.1
Sanitary Conditions	5	8.9
Weather	8	14.3
American Hostility	3	5.3
Vietnamese Impropriety	6	10.7
Lack of Freedom	5	8.9
Other Feelings	3	5.3
Standing in Chow Line	7	12.5
Total	56	100.0

Statements about the food were most often cited as reasons for their dislike of Camp Pendleton. A sample of the comments received: "Not used to American food." "The way Americans serve food. Food is not cooked and cold." "Food and lodging is not appropriate or suitable." "The food is not tasty." "Diet is not suitable. Rice is uncooked and meat is spoiled." "Food becomes scarce. Apples are too dry, not fresh."

There were 17.9 percent of the sample who disliked the food and another 12.5 percent who disliked standing in line for meals. More comments: "Dislike standing in line for food at noontime."

"Must stand in line under the sun at chow time." "Chow line too long in this camp, must wait for everything." "Must wait for food, would much rather cook own food."

Additional questions were then asked about the food and drink. First, to the question "Is the food suitable to your taste?" an overwhelming 72.9 percent said no. Ten percent found the food suitable and 16.9 percent stated it depended on the meals (See Table 60.) The quality of food was found to be good or very good by 19 percent of the respondents, fair by 44.8 percent of the sample, and not very good or not good at all by 36.2 percent of the respondents. (See Table 61.) In general, the quality of food was then judged by the Vietnamese to be less than good.

Table 60

IS THE FOOD SUITABLE TO YOUR TASTE?

	Frequency	Percentage
Yes	6	10.2
No	43	72.9
Some Are		
Some Are Not	10	17.9
Total	59	100.0

Table 61

QUALITY OF FOOD

	Frequency	Percentage
Very Good	2	3.4
Good	9	15.5
Fair	26	44.8
Not Very Good	16	27.6
Not Good At All	5	8.6
Total	59	100.0

The amount of food provided at mealtimes was adequate. (See Table 62.) The majority or 75.4 percent stated they always had enough food. Four respondents or 7 percent felt they never had enough food at mealtimes.

Table 62

AMOUNT OF FOOD

	Frequency	Percentage
Always Enough	43	75.4
Sometimes Enough	9	15.8
Never Enough	4	7.0
Other	1	1.8
No Response	2	
Total	59	100.0

To the question about drinking habits in Vietnam, the majority or 55.2 percent rarely or never drank. (See Table 63.) Only 13.8 percent drank almost daily and 12.1 percent drank sometimes weekly. Social drinkers numbered nine or 15.5 percent. As a group, the Vietnamese do not consume much alcohol.

Table 63

DRINKING FREQUENCY IN VIETNAM

	Frequency	Percentage
Almost Daily	8	13.8
Sometimes Weekly	7	12.1
Only Socially	9	15.5
Rarely or Never	32	55.2
Other	2	3.4
No Answer	1	
Total	59	100.0

The living conditions were disliked by 16.1 percent of the heads of households. Statements such as "lack convenience and comfort," "dislike living under the same tent with others," and "children were too noisy and disturbing" were given. The lack of sanitary conditions bothered another 8.9 percent of the Vietnamese. One stated they had "washing and bathing problems," and another stated dislike because they "must use public bathrooms and washrooms."

The weather conditions were disliked by eight Vietnamese respondents, who claimed it was either too hot, too cold, too sunny, windy or dusty. Phrases given by the respondents included: "Hot at noon, cold in the evening." "Too hot, Too sunny, windy and dusty." "Living quarters too cold." "Too hot in tent." "Live in cold and dusty tent."

Temperatures varied with the time of day and the type of living quarters.

There were six heads of households who remarked about the behavior of their fellow Vietnamese. There were some lifestyle clashes among different classes of Vietnamese. "Some Vietnamese are senseless or without dignity, therefore they degrade their own people." "Low level people from the rural class do not keep in line with American way." "Others' behavior not proper, for example, they are disorderly standing in the chow line."

The Vietnamese were not permitted to leave camp. This restriction was given by five Vietnamese as the reason they disliked Camp Pendleton. One stated he "felt not free," and wanted to "freely go out." There was no freedom to go out of camp and one head of household was anxious to "get out of camp and work my own way."

The way Americans treated them was disliked by three Vietnamese. One stated he was "mistreated by a few GI's," and another disliked the "arrogant manners of many Americans." Other Vietnamese found it difficult to accept American help because as stated by one Vietnamese he felt "disgusted having to ask help from someone who despises you." Different values and cultural backgrounds were observed by one head of household as the cause of discontent. He said, "the means by which help is mechanically provided are too numerous, yet the receiving end cannot still be satisfied due to different concepts and needs."

This comment recognizes the massive effort involved in setting up and maintaining the camp and its services. But types of difficulties for the Vietnamese also are apparent beyond such temporary complaints as the initial lack of clothing and educational and recreational facilities. A more general problem is the psychological state of the Vietnamese due to (1) their realistic needs; (2) the absence of their native culture and customary social networks; and (3) the basic tendency to psychological depression resulting from a camp environment.

Problems and criticisms of the refugee camps.—Some

specific self-criticisms were made by the Marines (USMC, 1975). They are perceptive but also reveal some shortcomings.

(1) Coordination of military and civilian lines of authority. This worked well on a personality basis on the whole but was not systematized.

(2) Accountability for refugees and their location. Suggestion was made by the Marines report for better control through its systems. One can ask here whether relocation within camp to be with relatives and friends might have been encouraged to rebuild social networks to renew or replace those disrupted by the refugee flight. Self-sorting into familial or social status groups is an organic development which should provide more psychological support and social control than a bureaucratic housing assignment which cannot take into account such sociological predispositions.

(3) Inexperienced food service contractors. (Little or no mention of continuity of the problem of food appealing to Vietnamese palates; rather the claim that this problem was solved.)

(4) Cultural differences, namely the use of open spaces for sanitary needs, washing of person and clothing in drinking fountains, tendency to offer bribes to security personnel. The conclusion of the Marine report under the topic of "inter-cultural adjustments" was that both refugees and the military or civilian staff be educated on a continuing basis as to cultural differences and that constant attention be directed toward maintaining a high level of sanitation and orderliness in the camps regardless of refugee inclinations (USMC, 1975, p. 47). This desire to change the Vietnamese sanitary habits would seem to be a rather limited recommendation given the possible problems and difficulties resulting for the Vietnamese in the failure of Americans to accommodate to some of their culture patterns. An assumption of one-way adjustment is evident and presumably not limited to sanitary problems.

(5) Inadequate clothing.

(6) Communication facilities.

(7) Utilization of refugees. Limited, as noted above.

(8) Leaving camp without authority, "more out of curiosity of the U.S. than anything else" (USMC, 1975, p. 51). Recommendation was for sterner action by Immigration and Naturalization Service, but what about a seemingly legitimate need to find out

more about the U.S.—an activity recommended by Navy psychiatrists in their consultation on behalf of children and adolescents? (Rahe and Looney, 1975)

(9) Proper assignment of a code name. This was most startling. It was listed as one of the major recommendations and problems!

Certainly concern and efficiency are indicated here, and some of the problems recognized indicated real sensitivity to the needs of the refugees. The military, however, was perhaps less aware of social and psychological needs as evidenced by lack of mention of mental problems or psychological adjustment, lack of interest in facilitating "community," as well as lack of sensitivity to difficulties of the Vietnamese in adjusting to a new culture.

Some specific criticisms have been made of overall administration of the refugee effort (Mineta, et. al., 1975). Initially, in the first two weeks of April, thirteen federal agencies were involved in the coordination and reception of refugees. Since not enough time was allowed to plan the operation, each of these agencies at first operated independently of each other and occasionally in conflict with each other, even after the establishment of the Interagency Task Force under the direction of first, Dean Brown, then Julia Vadala Taft. Some problems were experienced at the camp level at Camp Pendleton, but the confusion eventually was clarified and officials from the State Department assumed the highest authority. Congressman Mineta and his staff had many criticisms of overall coordination as well as some specifics.

"Because of the Task Force's composition—representing so many federal bureaucracies, each with its own concerns and goals—strong support from the President of the United States, as well as tough management by the Task Force's senior members, are necessary to prevent factional disagreements.

"Unfortunately, thus far, the President and the Task Force have provided only 'PR leadership' rather than 'authentic leadership.' The resettlement and evacuation efforts have been deficient in forceful managerial decisions and strong policy inception and implementation. As a result, there has been general mismanagement of financial and human resources, leading to the creation of a badly fragmented program.

"The Task Force has not fulfilled its responsibility in effectively coordinating and monitoring the program. It has failed to initiate and communicate positive directives to the various fed-

eral, state, and local governments and voluntary agencies. It has not kept comprehensive records on the refugees. And finally, it has failed to establish educational and acculturation programs inside and outside the camps which would adequately prepare the Cambodians and South Vietnamese for life in the United States. In other words, the Task Force has not used the money appropriated by Congress nor the personnel designated by numerous federal agencies in the most effective and efficient way." (Mineta et al, 1975:4-5)

Some support for Mineta's critical comments was provided by his investigation of the role of the Office of Management and Budget. The OMB appeared to be in a supervisory role over the Task Force, in spite of Mrs. Taft's denial (Mineta *et al.*, 1975, pp. 31-33), due to dissatisfaction with IATF administrative practices.

Specific detailed criticism offered by Mineta centered around the selection of individuals from various agencies to work in the camp who were not chosen by the camp coordinator. He had no control over the length of time such persons spent in the camp. This usually was a short period, resulting in rapid turnover. Because of the lack of authority of a civil coordinator, he had to depend on his personal charisma.

Mineta criticised the Department of Labor for some inadequacies in its services; i.e., failure to provide specific information about the job market and failure to maintain information on the employment status of the refugees for future guidance.

Mineta also disagreed with the Department of Health, Education, and Welfare point of view that the transitional nature of the camp did not permit comprehensive educational, vocational, and informational services, quoting a HEW Task Force official as saying that educational programs in the camp were "never designed to be good, nor were they established for any other purpose than to provide the refugees with a very basic acculturation curriculum" (Mineta *et al.*, 1975, p. 14). The Task Force considered the federal government's educational responsibility as limited; hence programs varied from camp to camp and were not extensive after departure from camp. Concern also was expressed by Mineta *et. al.* for regular curricula after September for school-age children, but relocation of most refugees took place before or soon after that date, obviating the problem.

Criticism was made by Mineta *et. al..* that in spite of recreational services in the camp, boredom was a problem and there was not sufficient professional guidance and counseling to cope with this as well as general depression.

While these and other specific criticisms can be made of the program and its overall coordination, considerable effort was mounted with some degree of functional accomplishment. Where it seems deficiencies existed in the U.S. effort, it seemed to be less the services in camp but rather in the understanding that "the receiving end cannot still be satisfied due to different concepts and needs." The most serious complaints to be made against the resettlement effort in the camps (and after): (1) lack of serious concern for mental health as opposed to material needs (2) assumption of a problem-free assimilation strategy in camp (and resettlement) (3) dispersal which in some cases involved break-up of extended families and lack of follow-up help and guidance; (4) lack of sensitivity in the camps to the cultural values and naturally occurring social network developments among refugees. The resettlement and sponsorship strategy will be discussed in the next section.

6
Mental Health

Against these distresses, the protection and the remedy most frequently advocated and ardently sought for is the presence of a native (Vietnamese) community. —Tran Minh Tung, M.D., former Vietnamese Health Minister, 1975

In comparison with all the immigrants from Europe and from Asia, the Vietnamese people were "sponsored" and scattered all over the country. Where is the Vietnamese community that they were looking for? Now, after two years, we wonder why there were so many mental health casualties. — William T. Liu, Ph.D., Director, Asian American Mental Health Research Center, 1977

When the personnel at Camp Pendleton were ready to receive refugees, they requested that the San Diego Navy Hospital take care of the health problems of refugees. After weeks of careful observations and consultations with Navy physicians at the camp's temporary dispensary, a conclusion was reached: "The general health of the Indochina refugees seems to be in every respect as good as that of the general population in this country" (United States Department of Health, Education, and Welfare, 1975:15).

The lack of disease symptoms, however, was not sufficient assurance that refugees were in good condition. Complaints of illness (or notable physical discomforts) were heard as days went by.

Early during the refugee assistance program, Segal and Lourie made a short inspection trip to Guam and other South Pacific islands. In their subsequent report to the National Institute of Mental Health assessing the mental health conditions of refugees en route to America, they stated:

"This concern reflects a recognition of the fact that throughout history, episodes involving the sudden uprooting and migration of a population have been accompanied by extreme and often lingering psychological and social stress. The Vietnamese refugees are certain to face a similarly broad range of both acute and chronic problems of adaptation and adjustment. Whether forced or voluntary, the precipitous departure from home and homeland is likely to evoke the anxiety and insecurity inherent in the new and unknown. The responses will often be reinforced by events; the sense of isolation and abandonment felt by many refugees will be heightened in the face of a predictable avalanche of family, social, vocational, and economic problems. The psychological history of refugee experience is marked by apathy and depression, bewilderment and panic, and disappointment and anger."—Segal and Lourie, 1975:2

In Camp Pendleton, Captain Rahe, Chief of the Stress Medicine Unit of the Naval Health Research Office in San Diego, observed:

"In all the camp areas, with the possible exception of Tent Area No. 5, we were impressed with the high level of morale and excellent psychological adjustment of the refugees to the immediate stresses of translocation. Children appeared playful and immensely adaptive to their new situation. Adults expressed more restrained enthusiasm but were cooperating with the many demands of refugee life."—Rahe, 1975a:2

Later at Camp Pendleton, refugee Vietnamese psychiatrist Dr. Tung, formerly Minister of Health of Thieu's Government, was frequently called upon as a consultant. He expressed concern for the mental health problems of the refugees and for a period of time operated a clinic on a volunteer basis to provide psychiatric services to the refugees.

Dr. Tung found at first, like Rahe, that the number of patients asking for psychiatric assistance was relatively small, although a perceptible deterioration was evident. Out of a camp of seventeen thousand, he saw from two to six patients a day and in four months hospitalized only 20. There were ten suicide attempts, one fatal. Daily patient load in the general purpose dispensary was also light, suggesting that "the complaints that could be related to psychological factors seemed less frequent than one could have expected in such circumstances" (Tung, 1975b, p. 3).

The limited case load seemed "paradoxical and contrary to all the predictions and even to the unanimous agreement among the refugees that their experience was definitely traumatic in many ways" (Tung, 1975b, p. 3). Tung explained it in terms of: (1) the physical inconvenience of going to the mental health center (at least one mile each way); (2) the Vietnamese tradition that views medicine as the domain of somatic disease and places non-physical problems outside the jurisdiction of a doctor. Vietnamese believe that sorrow and grief are "natural" and do not permit the sick role; (3) the special protection afforded by the camp; a "Vietnamese community complete with its neighborhood organization, its newspaper and even its daily pop music broadcast"; (4) the neutral climate in which persons are relieved of the normal responsibilities of daily living and shielded from reality; and finally, (5) a defense mechanism of denial and rationalization "to justify the rightfulness of the fateful decision that has changed the course of one's entire life. And as a consequence, not so many will be ready to acknowledge that one is suffering because one has chosen the wrong answer, and certainly not to the point of becoming a weakling and sick person" (Tung 1975, p. 4).

The first clients of the mental health clinic were thus chronic patients who were merely continuing the sick role that had been theirs in Vietnam; or those persons with a pre-existing illness or marginal adjustment who were experiencing psychotic breakdowns or relapses. Perhaps the trauma of the evacuation precipitated these occurrences, but it was not decisive in their formation.

"The rest and the majority of my patients presented signs of anxiety and depression, many of which could be labeled reactive or situational, with the reservation that the effect of stress is rarely evident in a direct manner. In most of these cases one may detect a previous neurotic pattern of behavior or the presence of long-standing inner conflicts that were revived or exacerbated by the present difficulties. Interestingly enough, nearly all the patients dated the appearance or resurgence of their symptoms

after they reached Camp Pendleton which put an end to their adventurous and often perilous escape. . . . In the suicidal cases the rate of stress appears more prominent, if not always with a direct bearing. In the only fatal suicide attempt a psychotic depression was precipitated in a Cambodian soldier by his grief over his mother whom he had left behind and his longing, mixed with fear, for repatriation. This dilemma, in fact, is the most crucifying bind for nearly all the refugees and the major reason for most suicides."—Tung 1975:4-5

Tung speaks of the "torturing bind" between staying in the U.S. and feeling lost from families and bearing the grief and guilt of abandoning families, conflicting with direct personal interests, especially the fear which opting for repatriation and gambling with one's life would entail. "For a single individual, this may lead to depression or to panic, and in the family, this is often the occasion of mutual reproach, the seed of discord and the source of more unhappiness" (Tung 1975, p. 9).

Tung points to some of the supportive factors in the social environment:

"*Against these distresses, the protection and the remedy most frequently advocated and ardently sought for is the presence of a native (Vietnamese) community. In that, of course, there is a vague expectation of solidarity and hope for assistance. But even if one needs no help and contemplates no close association with one's compatriots in the vicinity, the need of belonging is so profound that anything that contributes to ascertain that one is not alone is priceless. Hence comes the booming trade in all the camps of cassette tapes with recordings of Vietnamese popular music, which often are acquired at the cost of denying expenditures for other essential items. There comes also that glow of light that faultlessly appears at the mention of some Asian food shop or Chinatown, and not only because of the promises of gastronomical delights.*"—Tung, 1975:7

Conversely, if no support can be expected in the form of a liaison with friends or with compatriots, isolation intensifies the distress of traumatic experiences. Compounded by the sorrows of homesickness, by the remorse of having abandoned or failed loved ones, and by guilt for having deserted the homeland; it all adds up to the ingredients for a severe mental breakdown. The highest risk were men (sailors, airmen) and the rare women who had fled without their families and were sponsored out to live in some remote localities without a chance to relate to any fellow countrymen (Tung, 1975, pp. 7-8). Rahe also points to the camp "Vietnamese village" as a stabilizing factor for refugee mental health (Rahe, 1975a).

Besides isolation from fellow countrymen, Tung saw the absence of family as a major cause of mental health casualties, pointing out the size and strength of the Vietnamese family. The difficulty in escaping with such families:

"Was negated by the feeling of accomplishment and by a sense of force of security because one is giving and is also given love and protection. The head of household may have additional worry with heavier responsibility, but he also receives support and assistance from his dependents. The help in numerous cases is more than nominal and may consist in actual contribution to the family budget by the younger members of the family who often found a job more easily than the head of household with nontransferable skills. In the same vein, the wife and grandparents may suffer the pains of homesickness but very soon will fall into a regular, soothing routine within a familiar environment in which they are protected and need no adjustment."—Tung, 1975:8

Consideration was given by Dr. Tung and the naval psychiatrists to the special problems of children and adolescents as detailed in a report by Dr. Looney. Based on American research, he expected to find problems among six year olds and young adolescents, both groups "normally" (in American society) experiencing some natural separation from families. Here, however, cultural difference, especially the role of the family, was apparent.

"One is immediately impressed with a major difference between Vietnamese and American youth, particularly adolescents. That difference is the Vietnamese youths' strong sense of family solidarity. Large multi-generation families are the rule in the camps. Family members provide each other with great support. The teenagers are quite busy helping with the care of their younger siblings or aged relatives. They express a sense of feeling important and useful to their families. It is common to note teenagers and small children happily playing the same games, something not commonly seen in our society. This sense of purpose for the adolescents should help mitigate against the

development of boredom and its sequel—anti-social behavior. . . . The old people I interviewed appear in good spirits and feel useful in terms of helping with family chores. In these Vietnamese camps those young men who are heads of households appeared to me to constitute the group most consistently manifesting feelings of uselessness, futility, homesickness, and depression. These men, who were previously active and productive, now find themselves in a passive, inactive position. Their distress may well begin to erode the strength of the family and ultimately impose stress upon the youngsters. Fortunately for the children, the young mothers appeared busy and cheerful."—Looney, Consultation Report, May 20, 1975a:2-3

Of course, it is the male heads of household who have perhaps suffered the most role loss; in their work role especially, and perhaps to a degree as protectors and authority figures in the household.

All the refugees, of course, have suffered the loss—at one blow, to a greater or a lesser degree—of their customary social network: that complex of roles and interaction patterns played out by any given individual. In this sudden contraction of the social field—that stable and viable network of neighbors, employers, and kin—social positions were altered, norms were no longer relevant, relationships were *ad hoc* and temporary. The suddenness and the uncertainty of the refugee status greatly reduced the ability to reconstruct a viable and meaningful new field. Family groups or their remnants, and the Vietnamese "community" (or subcommunities) which might develop in camp were the rudiments of such reconstruction. In cases where both family and social network ties existed in the camp, administrators at times seemed to view them as a nuisance interfering with the bureaucratic routine of housing arrangements and location of records, rather than recognizing their essential contributions to the refugees' adjustment and well-being and their subsequent mental health.

Because of the transitory nature of the camp, patients did not undertake extensive therapy, but they were concerned about getting psychiatric assistance after leaving the camp and with problems of communication across the cultural barrier to be expected in such therapies.

"In any case, even under the most propitious circumstances,

the next few years will never be all smooth and easy. The job that has taken so long to find often is far from adequate in terms of pay or satisfaction. Communication is, at best, problematic and frequently the cause of distressing situations when a finer comprehension is essential, for example, in interpersonal relationships. There is yet to be a sense of belonging to the new homeland, and even with a degree of material success, one's family and one's own group of friends, a person often will wonder what good there is to live in this foreign country. And for the individual himself, familial conflicts and personal problems often become more intricate or more acute in this compulsory intimacy and dependency. A happy few may see it through with a great deal of luck and some degree of compliance and ingenuity. In most cases, this would not be a small feat. Whatever success that may obtain, there is a price to pay in exertion, in frustration, disquietude, mental disturbances and deviant behavior."—Tung 1975b:9

Tung predicts as a typical refugee pattern that:

"Most probably the unhappiness will be suffered in silence and in private; crying alone at night or just staying awake, remembering and regretting and feeling loneliness and emptiness. It could also account for vague symptoms, ascribed to one organ or the other, for then they could be regarded as legitimate reasons to ask for help. Disturbed behavior and acting out will not be too frequent due to the cultural inhibitions but may often cause intrafamilial problems."—Tung, 1975b:10

Tung goes on to discuss more severe manifestations of conversion hysteria and paranoid schizophrenia likely in Asians, particularly refugees who are cut off from normal communication because of the language barrier. A reality-based suspiciousness due to the political situation in Vietnam may also predispose the refugee to paranoia. He called for a large comprehensive program of assistance including data collection, regional centers, a training program for Vietnamese and Cambodians, education and information for both refugees and the general public to facilitate interacultural adjustment, and a coordinating body.

Stress: The psychological deterioration of "midway-to-nowhere."—Dr. Tung here, of course, is dealing not only with immediate problems and needs in the camp but more long-term mental health problems. With the passage of time Dr. Tung observed a gradual increase of mental health problems at Camp Pendelton; not so much grossly deviant behavior in the form of psychoses or suicides, but rather an increased number of patients coming to the clinic on their own with complaints of a more personal nature which fell into the categories of neuroses and psychophysiological disorders. While this change could be considered simply a measure of the greater acceptance of the clinic, Tung believed that given the traditional Vietnamese fear of not being discreet and stoical, admittance of an emotional problem needing consultation is undoubtedly a measure of the degree of suffering. "Grief and concern in this case seem to have gone beyond the level that could be borne in silence" (Tung, 1975b, p. 2). Dr. Tung noted more frequent diagnoses of anxiety and depression with symptoms so clear-cut as to be disturbing to the well-being of the patients. This was in contrast to an earlier series (June) when complaints were of a more minor nature, not interfering too much with patients' normal lives and in fact representing a healthy effort at adjustment.

"Depression, for example, is no longer described as mild downheartedness, but is characteristically tinted with feelings of hopelessness and guilt, and manifested by signs of psychomotor retardation."—Tung 1975b:3

Anxiety also differed in the latest series:

"Anxiety frequently is expressed in a most direct way and is described as a feeling state instead of being camouflaged as physical discomfort. As somatization has always been a common way of the Vietnamese neurotic patient to present his state of mental disarray, to admit the existence of this psychological problem could mean that the problem has become so prominent that it can no longer be ignored."—Tung 1975b:4

Suicide attempts, while still not many, increased from one in June to four in July. Tung also heard reports of an increasing number of violent or aggressive incidents, such as quarrels and fistfights.

Tung pointed out that stress had increased. By July, 1975, most refugees had experienced at least sixty days of fear, hardship, and boredom. The most recent arrivals were last-minute escapees with less preparation, who were more apt to be separated from families, who found more difficulties in obtaining sponsorship, and who were less educated and skilled.

The situation of deteriorating morale and mental health described by Dr. Tung, gives some substance to Kunz's description of the refugees in transit or interim camps, as being "midway to nowhere." "The longer he remains there, the longer he becomes subject to his demoralizing effects" (Kunz, 1973, p. 133). Dr. Tung observed, in his comment in August, "As we see it, the course has been downhill since July, and in probability will continue to deteriorate—necessitating some wise and timely interventions to prevent human tragedies—such as suicide" (Tung, 1975a, p. 7).

In spite of the superior health conditions of the refugee population in Camp Pendleton, numerous complaints of physical symptoms were observed through the collaborative monitoring efforts of the dispensary staff under Dr. Tung's direction, the naval psychiatrists, Captain Rahe, and Lt. Comm. Harold Ward, as well as the staff of the Asian American Mental Health Research Center under the direction of Dr. William Liu. The unusually high incidence of complaints of physical symptoms without bio-medical evidence was thought to be common for Asians who tend to somaticize their depressions and anxieties, a point which has been reported by many clinicians but which needs to be verified by health and psychiatric researchers. At any rate, the research staff was working on the hypothesis that major changes in one's life, such as loss of close relatives, changes of employment or becoming unemployed, and a change in residence, are important causes of physical stress which can result in illness.

To link major life events to physical illness, Rahe *et al*, in a series of papers ably demonstrated the utility of using the principle of optics to explain the impact of stress on illness (Rahe et al, 1974). While the notion that stress and physical illness are related in some way has been explored by anthropologists and sociologists, Rahe's model comes closest to the micro-theory which has the potential of precise predictive value which the macro-theories do not.

Rahe's assumption rests on the argument that both physical and psychological factors are contributory to the etiology of illness in the manner resembling the two sliding scales on a slide rule. In chronic illness such as coronary heart disease, diabetes, cancer, and multiple sclerosis, both slide scales are applicable, with etiological input coming from psychological stress as well as physical factors. Rahe also believes that stress is both a predisposing and precipitating factor in physical illness. To apply the optical theory, one may compare the sequence of events to a series of lenses and filters between a subject's exposure to recent life stress and his subsequent illness.

Briefly, life changes and illness are thought to be related, as they usually go hand-in-hand. If the life changes are plotted on a graph with illness clusters, they will coincide. The larger the life change, the more serious the predicted illness. Life changes may include job changes, marital status, births, deaths, and reunion of close relatives.

Rahe illustrated the model in terms of a series of optical lenses, with life stress indicated by light rays of various intensities. (See Figure 1.) First, there is the step one sorting filter where a person's past experiences may greatly influence his perception of a recent life change. In step two, the individual uses his ego defense mechanisms (such as denial) which may "diffract away" the impact of the event. On the other hand, if the event is not diffracted, it may bring about any of a number of psychophysiological responses in store in a "black box" (step three). If the person is aware of his problems, he may respond by being "depressed," or by experiencing "headaches" or muscle tension. Elevation of blood pressure and lipid level, or the lowering of blood glucose content may be the typical responses of those who are not aware of their problems. Step four suggests that some people find different ways to cope with their difficulties (e.g., physical exercises). But prolonged psychophysiological activation eventually leads to organic dysfunction and illness symptoms perceived by the individual even though medical personnel may not become aware of such problems. Such may become "illness behavior" as shown in step five. Finally, the sixth step is medical diagnosis.

The multitudes of drastic events and changes experienced by refugees from Vietnam offered an excellent opportunity to test the theory. A team of social scientists and three psychiatrists, including Dr. Tung, argued that the absence of organic basis notwithstanding, the refugee population would yield a high correlation between the severity and number of life change events and complaints about physical symptoms or morbid episodes. To validate the assumption, physical examination was supplemented by

the use of the Cornell Medical Index, which was designed to elicit data on anxiety, depression, and suicidal thoughts, in addition to physical symptoms. In commenting on the statistical profile of the index, Captain Rahe stated: "Of the randomly selected refugees (all interviewed in July, 1975) only three individuals had normal scores on the CMI. All the other 21 refugees showed grossly elevated scores—especially in regard to symptoms of severe anxiety and depression. A tendency was seen for the men to admit to greater deteriorization during their stay at Pendleton than the women."

The upper limit of total yes responses for the CMI questionnaire, determined from U.S. studies, is thirty. The upper limit of yes responses for the psychological sections of the CMI, sections M-R, is ten. Every one of the ten age and sex subgroups outlined above reported mean total yes responses above the thirty level. Women 20-29 years, 30-39 years, and 40-49 years showed highest levels—42, 46, and 44 yeses. Men 40-49 years showed the lowest mean level with 32 yeses. Boys 13-19 years and men 50+years showed the highest mean levels for males—42 and 44 yeses, respectively. When just the psychological scales on the Cornell Medical Index were examined, only women 20-29 years and 30-39 years had symptom levels greater than the upper limit; 11 yeses and 10.5 yeses, respectively. The only statistically significant difference between age-matched males and females was the higher psychological symptom level for women 20-29 years of age compared to men (t=2.50, p<.05). This is shown in Tables 64 and 65 respectively for males and females.

Rahe et al., (1977) analyzed data for males and females separately, with each sex divided into five age groups (Figure 2). Figure 2 presents RLCQ data from the standard list as well as from Vietnam war life changes. For most subgroups, the mean number of war-related life changes experienced over the six-month period immediately prior to leaving Vietnam were very similar (between two and four changes). The mean numbers of recent life changes reported on the standard list of the RLCQ, however, varied between subgroups (between two and eight changes). Men between the ages of 20-29 years and 30-39 years recorded the greatest mean number of war-related plus standard recent life changes (nearly 12 changes). Lowest mean totals for both categories of recent life changes were recorded by women

40-49 years and 50+ years of age (between four and five changes).

Noting the various changes that an average refugee had experienced prior to the exodus, one would be led to believe that at least the war experience was now over and a new life was beginning. Indeed many respondents felt relieved in spite of the various complaints about their family separations and the uncertainty of their immediate plans. Refugees, although anxious to leave the camp and find sympathetic sponsors, were overwhelmed by the anticipation of a separation from their fellow countrymen. A substantial number even expressed their unwillingness to leave the camp. The widespread feelings of refugees desiring to stay in the camp was noted in August when the *New York Times* quoted one top civilian officer as saying refugees were suffering from *campitis* or the fear to enter into a life with unknown surroundings. Some of the older Japanese Americans recalled a similar situation occurred during World War II when incarcerated Japanese Americans had already developed a feeling of togetherness in the camps.

The morale of refugees must be measured against their expectations about the future, rather than solely on their immediate experience in the camp. One civilian officer in the camp remarked that the undesirable living conditions were perhaps intended and even desirable from the viewpoints of the program objectives. They argued that refugees must be encouraged to think of a better life outside the camp and thus wish to leave the camp.

Assessment of the present and perceptions of the future.— After the long journey, having just lost a permanent home, employment, or business, and separated from family members, the refugee would likely be at the lowest emotional state when interviewed at Camp Pendleton. But many probably felt the worst of the uncertainty was over compared with the conditions of a worn out government and complete military collapse. But the low point was expected to be a transient phenomenon. The psychological condition of the refugees was not to be evaluated as if it could become an ongoing condition, greatly influencing the well-being of the entire group in the months and years to come.

In order to get at the time perspective of the morale problem, the investigators used a measure first devised some twenty years ago by Hadley Cantril of Princeton University. Briefly, the mea-

Table 64

Cornell Medical Index
(Males)

	13-19 yrs.		20-29 yrs.		30-39 yrs.		40-49 yrs.		50+ yrs.	
	Mean	S.D.	Mean	S.D.	Mean	S.D.	Mean	S.D.	Mean	S.D.
Number of males	32		25		12		21		9	
Section A: Ears/Eyes										
Events in Vietnam	1.1	1.5	1.2	1.9	1.3	1.8	2.0	1.8	2.2	2.0
Events in camp	1.0	1.2	1.4	1.9	.9	1.0	2.0	1.9	2.1	2.2
Section B: Respiratory										
Events in Vietnam	2.4	2.1	2.2	2.2	2.5	3.1	1.8	2.0	2.3	2.8
Events in camp	1.5	1.7	1.6	1.8	1.2	1.6	1.0	2.0	3.6	3.1
Section C: Cardiovascular										
Events in Vietnam	2.0	1.9	1.8	2.0	1.0	1.2	2.9	1.8	2.1	2.7
Events in camp	1.2	1.6	1.4	1.8	.5	.6	2.5	1.6	2.2	2.7
Section D: Digestive										
Events in Vietnam	3.0	2.6	3.2	3.6	3.2	3.7	1.2	2.4	5.0	3.2
Events in camp	1.8	2.4	2.7	2.6	1.6	2.0	.7	2.2	3.4	3.4
Section E: Musculo-skeletal										
Events in Vietnam	.9	1.2	.6	.9	.6	1.0	1.2	1.8	2.4	2.0
Events in camp	.8	1.2	.3	.6	.3	.6	1.1	1.0	2.1	2.2
Section F: Skin										
Events in Vietnam	1.9	1.8	1.4	1.2	1.3	1.5	2.1	1.5	1.8	1.0
Events in camp	1.2	1.6	.9	1.2	.6	1.2	.8	1.2	1.6	1.6
Section G: Nervous system										
Events in Vietnam	2.4	2.2	2.2	2.2	2.8	1.6	1.1	2.6	2.1	2.5
Events in camp	1.3	2.0	.8	1.4	.8	1.4	.8	1.5	2.6	3.0
Section H: Genito-urinary										
Events in Vietnam	.8	1.0	1.4	1.7	2.2	2.3	1.0	1.6	1.6	1.2
Events in camp	.4	.7	.6	1.1	.6	.8	.2	1.2	1.2	2.0
Section I: Fatigability										
Events in Vietnam	.8	1.2	1.1	1.6	1.4	1.6	.8	1.6	1.2	1.7
Events in camp	.9	1.4	.6	.8	.8	1.0	.4	.6	.8	1.6
Section J: Frequency of illness										
Events in Vietnam	1.2	1.5	.8	1.2	.8	1.0	1.4	1.4	2.1	2.5
Events in camp	.8	1.3	.4	.6	.5	.8	.3	1.0	2.3	2.6
Section K: Miscellaneous										
Events in Vietnam	1.2	1.3	1.4	1.2	2.0	1.2	1.8	1.4	2.8	2.4
Events in camp	.2	.5	.3	.6	.5	1.2	.8	.7	.8	1.4
Section L: Habits										
Events in Vietnam	.9	1.0	1.4	1.7	1.2	1.2	1.4	1.1	1.8	1.6
Events in camp	.8	.8	1.0	1.4	.8	1.2	.8	1.1	1.8	1.7

	13-19 years			20-29 years			30-39 years			40-49 years			50+ years		
	Mean	S.D.	N	Mean	S.D.	N	Mean	S.D.	N	Mean	S.D.	N	Mean	S.D.	N
Section M: Inadequacy															
Events in Vietnam	3.6	2.8		3.9	2.8		2.4	2.0		2.4	2.4		2.2	2.6	
Events in camp	2.3	2.4		1.4	1.8		1.0	1.8		1.0	1.6		2.0	2.6	
Section N: Depression															
Events in Vietnam	.8	1.2		.4	.8		1.2	1.5		.2	.5		.6	1.3	
Events in camp	.9	1.4		.6	1.0		.8	.8		.2	.5		1.1	1.6	
Section O: Anxiety															
Events in Vietnam	1.7	1.5		1.8	1.6		1.8	1.8		1.2	1.4		.8	1.0	
Events in camp	1.2	1.2		.5	.8		1.3	1.6		.8	1.4		1.1	1.5	
Section P: Sensitivity															
Events in Vietnam	2.0	1.6		1.8	1.8		2.2	1.6		1.5	1.6		1.4	1.9	
Events in camp	1.4	1.6		.5	1.0		1.2	1.5		.8	1.4		1.3	1.9	
Section Q: Anger															
Events in Vietnam	2.8	2.2		3.0	2.6		3.0	2.0		2.4	2.9		2.6	3.0	
Events in camp	1.8	1.9		1.3	1.6		1.8	2.4		.7	1.8		2.2	3.2	
Section R: Tension															
Events in Vietnam	2.2	2.0		1.2	1.8		.6	.8		1.2	1.8		1.3	1.8	
Events in camp	1.4	2.2		.4	1.2		.2	.4		.6	1.6		1.3	2.6	
Sections I & J															
Events in Vietnam	2.0	2.4		1.8	2.4		2.2	2.4		1.8	2.8		3.3	3.6	
Events in camp	1.8	2.4		1.0	1.2		1.2	1.4		.6	1.2		3.2	4.0	
Section M-R															
Events in Vietnam	13.4	9.3		12.2	8.6		11.2	6.6		9.1	9.0		8.8	10.3	
Events in camp	9.0	0.9		4.8	4.3		6.3	6.1		4.0	7.4		9.1	12.8	
Total CMI															
Events in Vietnam	32.2	20.8		31.3	20.0		31.6	19.6		28.1	19.6		36.6	26.8	
Events in camp	21.1	19.0		17.3	13.6		15.4	12.3		16.4	14.1		33.3	33.3	
Total events	44.6	22.6		37.2	21.8		35.3	18.3		32.6	19.4		46.2	35.2	
Life Change – Adjustment (68–79)															
Items checked	2.9	3.0	32	4.6	5.5	25	1.6	2.2	12	4.4	5.3	21	6.0	3.1	9
Subjective score	44.8	29.1	13	106.2	79.1	8	48.5	55.8	2	73.8	37.8	7	91.8	33.8	5
Life Change – Anticipated (80–97)															
Items checked	7.4	3.6	32	10.3	5.1	25	6.6	4.8	12	8.8	4.7	21	8.8	3.6	9
Subjective score	76.0	41.1	21	114.2	68.0	16	80.1	64.0	7	89.8	40.8	11	115.2	43.2	6

Table 65

CORNELL MEDICAL INDEX SCORES
(Females)

	13-19 yrs. Mean	S.D.	20-29 yrs. Mean	S.D.	30-39 yrs. Mean	S.D.	40-49 yrs. Mean	S.D.	50+ yrs. Mean	S.D.
Number of females	31		24		25		13		11	
Section A: Ears/Eyes										
Events in Vietnam	.2	.7	.6	.9	1.6	1.7	2.8	2.6	2.4	1.6
Events in camp	.7	1.0	.8	1.1	1.6	2.0	3.0	2.7	1.9	1.8
Section B: Respiratory										
Events in Vietnam	1.8	2.0	2.1	2.8	2.0	2.6	2.2	2.2	2.4	2.0
Events in camp	2.2	2.4	2.8	3.4	2.9	2.8	3.4	2.8	2.0	2.2
Section C: Cardiovascular										
Events in Vietnam	1.3	1.8	2.1	2.6	2.8	2.4	1.6	1.8	1.0	1.0
Events in camp	1.2	2.2	2.2	2.5	2.0	2.4	2.2	2.6	.8	1.0
Section D: Digestive										
Events in Vietnam	2.7	3.6	3.2	3.4	3.0	2.3	3.3	3.4	3.2	3.0
Events in camp	2.8	3.0	3.6	3.2	2.6	2.4	4.4	3.8	2.2	3.2
Section E: Musculo-skeletal										
Events in Vietnam	.8	1.4	1.6	1.8	1.1	1.5	1.6	1.8	3.0	1.8
Events in camp	.7	1.0	1.2	1.7	1.4	2.0	1.8	1.7	.12	1.8
Section F: Skin										
Events in Vietnam	1.1	1.4	1.2	1.3	1.2	1.4	1.0	1.0	1.0	1.1
Events in camp	1.2	1.2	1.4	1.4	1.0	1.3	1.2	1.3	.8	1.0
Section G: Nervous system										
Events in Vietnam	2.0	2.2	2.3	2.5	2.4	2.4	3.2	3.0	3.2	2.8
Events in camp	1.6	2.0	2.2	2.5	2.4	2.2	2.2	2.2	1.6	2.4
Section H: Genito-urinary										
Events in Vietnam	1.7	1.8	2.4	2.2	1.6	1.6	1.5	1.8	.7	1.2
Events in camp	1.4	1.8	1.7	2.0	1.2	1.6	1.3	1.9	.4	.9
Section I: Fatigability										
Events in Vietnam	1.0	1.5	1.1	1.7	1.0	1.5	.9	1.2	2.0	1.8
Events in camp	.7	1.1	1.3	1.8	1.2	1.7	1.4	1.4	.7	1.0
Section J: Frequency of illness										
Events in Vietnam	.6	1.6	1.4	2.4	1.2	2.4	1.2	2.0	.8	1.4
Events in camp	.4	1.2	1.6	2.4	1.7	2.6	2.2	2.5	1.4	2.2

Section K: Miscellaneous										
Events in Vietnam	1.1	1.9	1.2	1.8	1.4	1.8	1.0	1.0	1.3	.6
Events in camp	.3	.0	.4	.3	.8	.6	1.2	.5	.6	.2
Section L: Habits										
Events in Vietnam	1.2	.9	.8	.8	1.0	1.0	1.0	.8	.5	.3
Events in camp	.8	.4	.9	.8	1.1	1.4	1.0	.8	.8	.6
Section M: Inadequacy										
Events in Vietnam	2.4	2.9	3.0	4.4	3.4	5.2	2.9	3.0	3.5	4.1
Events in camp	1.7	1.0	3.2	2.4	3.2	2.8	2.6	2.0	2.1	1.9
Section N: Depression										
Events in Vietnam	1.4	1.0	.9	.6	1.6	1.2	1.3	.9	2.2	1.2
Events in camp	1.6	1.0	1.3	1.8	1.8	1.6	1.8	1.4	1.7	1.0
Section O: Anxiety										
Events in Vietnam	1.6	1.4	1.0	1.4	1.5	1.6	1.6	1.6	1.6	1.2
Events in camp	1.7	1.2	1.0	1.2	1.4	1.2	2.0	1.5	1.3	.8
Section P: Sensitivity										
Events in Vietnam	1.6	2.7	2.0	1.9	1.8	2.2	1.8	2.4	1.8	1.8
Events in camp	1.6	1.2	1.8	1.2	1.3	1.2	1.7	1.6	1.5	1.2
Section Q: Anger										
Events in Vietnam	2.4	2.7	2.0	2.4	2.4	3.0	2.9	3.0	2.3	2.4
Events in camp	1.8	1.2	2.6	1.6	2.6	2.0	2.8	2.6	1.8	1.2
Section R: Tension										
Events in Vietnam	2.4	2.8	1.9	2.8	2.6	2.9	2.4	2.2	2.4	2.5
Events in camp	1.5	.8	1.3	1.6	2.4	1.7	2.6	2.0	1.9	1.4
Sections I & J										
Events in Vietnam	3.1	2.9	3.0	2.0	3.7	2.2	4.0	2.5	2.8	1.6
Events in camp	2.8	2.0	3.6	3.5	4.2	3.0	4.1	2.9	1.9	1.2
Section M-R										
Events in Vietnam	9.0	13.6	8.8	13.6	10.4	16.2	10.8	13.3	11.3	13.4
Events in camp	8.7	6.6	8.4	9.9	10.7	10.6	11.2	11.2	7.9	7.8
Total CMI										
Events in Vietnam	19.4	36.6	25.0	35.8	22.2	37.3	26.4	32.8	22.8	27.9
Events in camp	20.6	20.4	24.1	34.0	25.8	30.6	26.5	30.6	15.8	21.9
Total events	24.9	42.2	29.0	48.5	25.8	49.6	30.8	44.6	20.4	37.4

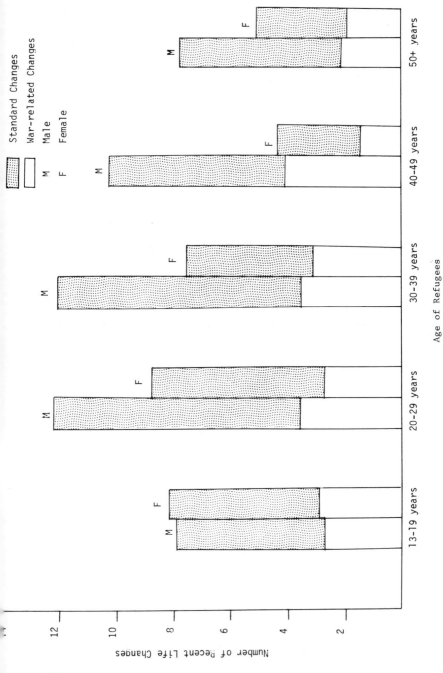

Number of Recent Life Changes

Age of Refugees

Standard Changes
War-related Changes
M Male
F Female

Table 66

VIETNAMESE REFUGEE STUDY: RECENT LIFE CHANGES QUESTIONNAIRE
(Males)

	13-19 years Mean	S.D.	N	20-29 years Mean	S.D.	N	30-39 years Mean	S.D.	N	40-49 years Mean	S.D.	N	50+ years Mean	S.D.	N
Life Change - Standard (1-55)															
1-6 mos. - checked	5.1	5.0	32	8.6	6.4	25	8.5	5.2	12	6.1	3.8	21	5.6	5.6	9
7-12 mos. - checked	1.0	1.6	32	2.5	3.2	25	2.0	2.0	12	1.6	2.6	21	2.0	1.6	9
13-18 mos. - checked	.4	1.0	32	1.2	1.4	24	1.8	2.6	12	1.8	2.1	21	3.1	2.0	9
19-24 mos. - checked	1.3	2.4	32	2.0	2.8	25	1.4	1.8	12	2.4	2.8	21	2.4	1.8	9
1-6 mos. - subjective score	48.7	50.0	26	92.8	61.6	25	88.0	60.1	12	67.8	49.7	20	70.6	80.9	9
7-12 mos. subj. score	17.4	11.1	14	38.0	32.0	25	27.8	25.5	9	23.1	33.6	14	29.4	16.6	7
13-18 mos. - subj. score	20.1	18.2	7	16.5	12.2	14	35.5	21.7	6	26.0	30.0	13	35.6	18.7	8
19-24 mos. - subj. score	29.7	33.2	10	31.4	35.2	16	32.8	21.2	6	33.0	34.4	15	30.7	17.7	7
Life Change— War Experience (56-67)															
1-6 mos. - checked	2.8	3.0	32	3.6	3.2	25	3.6	2.6	12	4.2	3.4	21	2.2	2.2	9
7-12 mos. - checked	.8	1.9	32	.9	1.2	25	.8	2.6	12	.6	1.1	21	.6	.7	9
13-18 mos. - checked	.3	1.4	32	.5	1.0	24	.0	.2	12	.6	1.0	21	.8	1.6	9
19-24 mos. - checked	.6	1.6	32	1.8	2.4	25	.8	1.4	9	1.0	1.4	21	1.4	2.4	7
1-6 mos. - subjective score	41.2	44.5	19	43.4	32.3	20	54.0	39.8	9	49.5	38.8	6	37.6	39.6	5
7-12 mos. - subj. score	23.8	37.9	9	19.2	11.4	12	45.5	58.6	2	20.2	17.4	7	13.6	6.2	3
13-18 mos. - subj. score	7.0	1.4	2	22.0	6.4	5	4.0	0.0	1	20.2	19.2	8	26.6	16.2	4
19-24 mos. - subj. score	12.3	7.6	6	26.1	28.5	16	12.0	8.7	3	22.8	21.0		42.2	30.8	
Life Change - Evacuation (68-79)															
Items checked	7.4	4.6	32	11.0	4.4	25	8.9	4.8	12	9.4	5.4	21	8.8	4.8	9
Subjective score	45.0	28.9	21	114.2	59.5	15	95.8	106.5	7	90.8	67.2	11	91.2	35.8	5
Life Change - War (1-6 mos) & Evacuation (68-79)															
Items checked	10.2	5.8	32	14.5	6.2	25	12.6	6.7	12	13.7	7.1	21	11.1	4.0	9
Subjective score	92.0	70.8	14	157.9	74.4	12	156.7	127.3	7	142.6	87.2	11	151.8	41.7	4

VIETNAMESE REFUGEE STUDY: RECENT LIFE CHANGES QUESTIONNAIRE

Females

	13-19 years Mean	S.D.	N	20-29 years Mean	S.D.	N	30-39 years Mean	S.D.	N	40-49 years Mean	S.D.	N	50+ years Mean	S.D.	N
Life Change - Standard (1-55)															
1-6 mos. - checked	5.2	3.9	31	6.0	4.7	24	4.4	4.0	25	2.9	1.9	13	3.2	2.4	11
7-12 mos. - checked	.7	1.2	31	1.7	1.8	24	1.2	1.0	25	.6	.8	13	.8	1.2	11
13-18 mos. - checked	.7	1.6	31	.8	.9	24	.7	.8	25	1.2	1.4	13	1.0	1.2	11
19-24 mos. - checked	.5	.9	31	1.2	2.2	24	2.2	2.2	25	.8	1.0	13	1.9	2.0	11
1-6 mos. - subjective score	48.8	36.0	25	76.5	71.4	22	64.1	68.4	20	34.8	20.6	12	33.4	20.6	8
7-12 mos. - subj. score	18.7	8.6	10	36.2	25.2	14	17.9	7.8	18	16.3	5.6	6	15.6	6.6	5
13-18 mos. - subj. score	27.8	29.6	10	22.2	15.6	11	15.2	7.2	13	21.2	9.4	7	23.4	20.2	5
19-24 mos. - subj. score	22.1	12.6	10	39.2	33.0	8	37.9	31.6	17	19.6	13.8	6	38.2	24.8	5
Life Change - War Experience (56-67)															
1-6 mos. - checked	3.0	3.0	31	2.8	3.6	24	3.2	2.7	25	1.5	1.4	13	1.9	1.8	11
7-12 mos. - checked	.4	.9	31	.9	2.1	24	.4	.8	25	.3	.8	13	.2	.6	11
13-18 mos. - checked	.2	.4	31	.2	.6	24	.2	.5	25	.2	.4	13	.4	.6	11
19-24 mos. - checked	.0	.4	31	.5	.9	24	.4	.9	25	.0	.2	13	.6	1.0	11
1-6 mos. - subj. score	36.6	31.1	21	45.6	56.0	18	49.2	44.4	23	36.8	21.3	8	14.8	11.6	9
7-12 mos. - subj. score	12.6	12.7	5	28.0	34.2	9	10.3	8.7	6	20.0	14.1	2	13.0	4.2	2
13-18 mos. - subj. score	18.5	9.9	4	17.8	9.2	4	18.3	5.8	3	17.0	1.4	2	6.3	5.8	3
19-24 mos. - subj. score	4.5	.7	2	20.2	21.0	2	17.8	5.2	7	20.0	0.0	1	7.6	6.1	3
Life Change - Evacuation (68-79)															
Items checked	7.6	4.7	31	10.5	4.3	24	9.3	4.6	25	7.8	6.2	13	10.0	3.4	11
Subjective score	81.7	50.0	15	106.5	52.4	7	110.0	88.8	8	35.0	0.0	1	84.3	61.4	3

	13-19 years Mean	S.D.	N	20-29 years Mean	S.D.	N	30-39 years Mean	S.D.	N	40-49 years Mean	S.D.	N	50+ years Mean	S.D.	N
Life Change - War (1-6 mos.)															
Evacuation (68-79)															
Items checked	10.0	5.6	31	13.2	6.3	24	12.6	6.4	25	9.4	7.0	25	11.9	4.0	11
Subjective score	118.8	59.0	12	141.7	63.8	7	180.9	125.0	13	115.0	0.0	14	97.3	68.4	3
Life Change - Adjustment (68-79)															
Items checked	4.8	4.7	31	6.4	5.4	24	5.4	5.1	25	7.0	6.0	7	3.4	4.2	11
Subjective score	59.9	54.0	12	98.6	42.9	7	57.6	68.9	8	-	-	-	39.0	0.0	1
Life Change - Anticipated (80-97)															
Items checked	7.8	5.1	31	10.4	5.2	24	8.8	4.6	25	9.9	6.4	25	5.4	4.4	11
Subjective score	72.5	41.0	18	87.2	49.6	11	76.8	64.4	13	46.6	11.5	13	29.0	7.0	2

sure consists of a figure of a ladder with several steps. The respondent is asked to simply place himself or herself on the various steps of the ladder to indicate just where he or she finds herself in terms of life status at various time intervals (e.g., in the past five years, at present, or in the next few years). (See Table 68.)

Figures 3 and 4 show three age groups for both men and women: 13-19 years, 20-39 years, and 40+ years of age. In Figure 3, teenage boys showed lowest life status ratings for one and five years ago (in Vietnam) and highest anticipated life status ratings for one to five years in the future (in America). On the other hand, the oldest male group exhibited highest life status ratings in Vietnam. The contrast of the two age groups reflected the pain of the loss by the mature adult male who lost everything as a result of the evacuation as compared with the teen-age group who by and large had little to lose, and were looking forward to opportunities which the old country was unable to offer. For the younger age group, this was a new beginning and they were anxious to explore the new world. For the older male group, the old norms and social status had crumbled, their stable image was expected to change and the new norms were not formed. For most, such a sudden change could be more difficult for them to handle as compared with the younger group of both sexes.

In Figure 4, the youngest women reported highest life status ratings which only in part paralleled the male counterpart; and the oldest women had the lowest life status ratings. The relatively low status ratings for the oldest women were in marked contrast to the higher ratings made by men in the same age group for all time periods. But in terms of time perspective, both men and women in all groups indicated lowest life status ratings for their camp experience.

Some significant findings were noted when age, life change, and physical symptoms were seen together. First, women between 20 and 39 years of age reported more psychological symptoms to psychiatrists who monitored their problems in Camp Pendleton. From physicians' reports, the same age group also reported to have an unusually high incidence of menstrual irregularities. On the other hand, men between 20 and 39 years of age reported the largest number of recent life changes, but reported little or the lowest incidences of morbid symptoms normally expected to accompany such life changes.

139

Table 68

VIETNAMESE REFUGEE STUDY: SELF ANCHORING SCALE

Males

	13-19 yrs. N = 32		20-29 yrs. N = 25		30-39 yrs. N = 12		40-49 yrs. N = 21		50+ yrs. N = 9	
	Mean	S.D.	Mean	S.D.	Mean	S.D.	Mean	S.D.	Mean	S.D.
Number of males										
5 years ago	10.5	5.0	10.6	3.3	12.0	4.3	13.6	4.2	12.2	4.6
1 year ago	11.8	4.9	12.6	3.4	13.6	4.2	15.7	3.1	13.8	4.6
Now	9.1	4.0	7.0	4.2	6.5	4.2	9.0	4.2	7.6	3.2
Now (if expectations true)	14.7	4.0	13.2	4.4	14.7	4.4	14.2	3.6	13.0	4.2
1 year from now	15.9	3.4	14.4	3.5	14.6	5.0	15.6	2.8	14.8	3.6
5 years from now	17.5	2.8	15.5	3.9	16.1	4.6	17.3	2.5	16.8	6.5

Females

	13-19 yrs. N = 31		20-29 yrs. N = 24		30-39 yrs. N = 25		40-49 yrs. N = 13		50+ yrs. N = 11	
	Mean	S.D.	Mean	S.D.	Mean	S.D.	Mean	S.D.	Mean	S.D.
Number of females										
5 years ago	13.0	5.6	12.8	4.2	12.6	4.0	12.2	3.4	11.2	4.4
1 year ago	13.8	5.0	13.8	3.6	12.8	5.9	11.8	3.4	12.0	5.6
Now	8.4	3.8	6.4	3.6	7.3	5.1	4.6	4.8	7.2	4.8
Now (if expectations true)	15.2	3.8	14.8	3.2	13.4	4.3	9.8	5.0	11.0	5.4
1 year from now	16.7	3.4	15.8	3.0	14.2	3.8	11.0	4.0	11.4	5.2
5 years from now	17.8	2.8	17.5	2.6	16.2	3.2	12.7	3.6	12.9	5.4

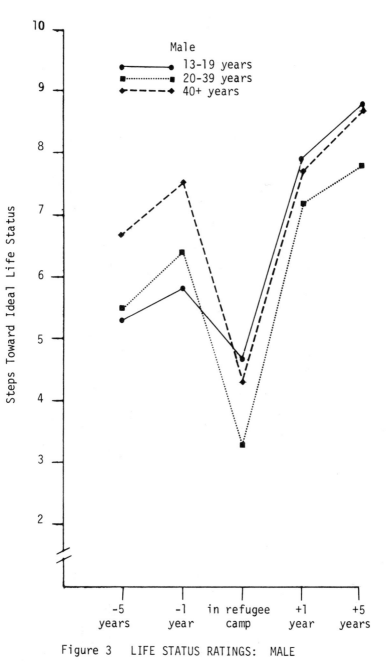

Figure 3   LIFE STATUS RATINGS: MALE

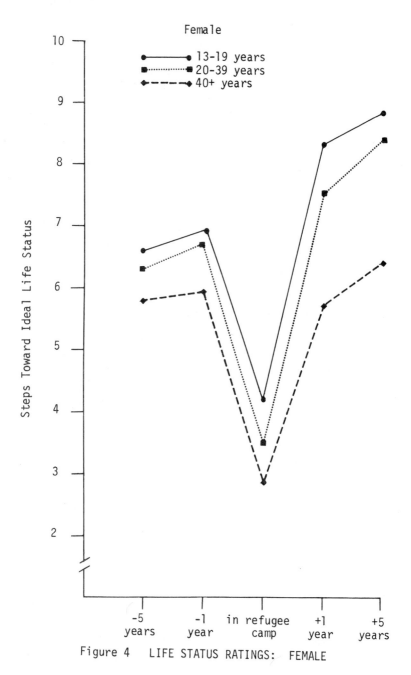

Figure 4   LIFE STATUS RATINGS: FEMALE

The frequency of life change scores for men in the 20-39 years of age group was, however, found to be related to their views of their life status ratings. This group, which reported the highest frequency of life changes also reported the lowest point of their life status as being the time they were in Camp.

In any event, Table 68, which gives the mean scores of all respondents in their perceived life status ratings, shows that all age groups had high aspirations for a better life in America one year from the time they were interviewed in 1975; the expectation of a much better life five years from the time of the interview was expected by all, in contrast with what they had experienced over the past five years. Among women 40-49 years of age and those over 50 years of age, the contrast between five years ago and the next five years was somewhat less discernible. In 1975, the most encouraging sign was the fact that all refugees, regardless of social class, age, or sex were looking forward to a better life. Such expectations may have been one of the major positive factors in the subsequent adjustment of many refugees and their willingness to solve their own problems. On the other hand, it was precisely because of such high expectations that many became disillusioned by the harsh realities of unemployment, or underemployment when that time finally came.

It is necessary for refugees, while in camp, to view their future hopefully, with a sense of beginning a new life once they are out of the camp. Without such aspirations, depression and even suicides would have been much more noticeable in Camp Pendleton between May and December of 1975. Thus, the comparative assessment of the life status ratings by refugees was a good indication of their optimistic notes. On the other hand, high expectations beyond the realm of realistic situations outside the camp could be a problem in the long run, as many found out three years after the resettlement. The press and other media at one time had selected mostly successful cases to report, thus creating a sense of relative deprivation for the many refugees who remained unemployed, or had a hard time. In any case, perhaps for many the optimistic expectations during the days when they were in Camp Pendleton had more positive impact on them than the disappointment which was created by the high expectations.

The assessment of life changes and mental health (as well as physical well-being) did yield some significant results, though the statistical data needs to be more carefully studied against other variables for many months in the future. In general, however, both age and sex of the respondent are important variables related to the symptoms produced by realities of recent life changes, particularly those related to the recent war experience.

Health conditions: Disease or illness?—The experience of refugees in Camp Pendleton and the efforts by the naval medical personnel yielded an important, though perhaps somewhat less clear, piece of information. Recalling the Department of Health, Education and Welfare Report (1975) about the excellent health conditions of refugees in the Camp, which contrasted with complaints made by refugees themselves through the check lists of the Cornell Medical Index, there appeared to be some unexplainable discrepencies. The discrepencies suggested that physicians and para-medical personnel in the dispensary judged the health condition of refugees in terms of negative findings, or the absence of disease entities. On the other hand, refugees tended to report their health conditions in terms of self-defined morbid episodes. These morbid episodes may be natural occurrences when the individual has departed from his/her normal routines, has to take food to which he is unaccustomed, or experiences sudden climate change for which he has little to protect his body temperature, as was the case at Camp Pendleton. On the cultural level, morbid episodes may simply be an expression of what the western medical system would normally regard as symptoms of depression, anxiety and anger. Since there are no culturally appropriate expressions for such behavior in terms of mental health concepts in most non-western cultures, victims either offered explanations on the causes of such complaints which made little difference to western medicine professionals, or translated such symptoms into physical terms, with little or no organic basis. (In consultation with psychiatrists from Asia and with Dr. Tung, this point was substantiated by practitioners among Asian patients. The second phase of this study will focus on some of these assumptions in 1978-79.)

7
Unaccompanied Children

Vietnamese, like all people, do not want to lose their children. All Vietnamese have a strong sense of family obligation, and they have shown themselves willing and capable of caring for their own children. Our great moral responsibility is to enable them, in their time of great tragedy, to do so.—
Joseph Reid, executive director of the Child Welfare League of America, quoted in *Denver Post*, April 9, 1975

During the mass evacuation in the final days of Thieu's government, amidst the confusion, many children left Vietnam without parents, and some without even close relatives. It later became clear that a substantial number of the "unaccompanied children," as they were labeled, were trusted to friends and relatives who could leave the country. Others without relatives became acquainted with some families *en route* to the camp. During the registration a good portion of the unaccompanied children were included in family rosters as a part of the extended family. The situation worked out well for these unaccompanied children; those who registered them as members of their families had, in fact, become their foster parents and relatives, a situation quite common during the war-torn years in Vietnam. However, as these families registered to be sponsored out of the camp, the identities of the unaccompanied children were revealed.

In early May of 1975, the social science team who helped to monitor the health and mental health conditions in camp learned of the existence of those unaccompanied children, even though the exact number remained unclear. Staff of the research team took extra precaution to keep the information secret in order to minimize adverse publicity.

Refugee camps created as a result of international and national political and military activities are most vulnerable to criticism. On an average day some four hundred media people combed through the camp site for newsworthy stories.

Dr. John G. Looney, the Child and Adolescent Psychiatrist member of the mental health consultation team from the Naval Health Research Center, quietly and earnestly evaluated the mental health conditions of the unaccompanied children twice in June and once in July, 1975. At the time of his first visit, he identified thirteen children who were totally without friends or relatives in the camp. These children were later relocated, grouped together in a tent in Camp Four. Stories began to circulate about these children. One story explained that the unaccompanied children must be carefully isolated from the public because their unusual status made them vulnerable to exploitation by the media and others who were not sympathetic to the whole evacuation plan. Another story focused on the fact that the unaccompanied children were in fact ridiculed by other children in the camp and were called "bastards." To avoid further hardship, the Marine Corps authority was said to have made the decision to place them together. In view of the situation at that time, if indeed the extra efforts were made to protect the welfare of these unaccompanied children, this was commendable. Stories continued to circulate, however, and it raises the question as to whose interests were served by the relocation of the unaccompanied children.

In Dr. Looney's first visit report, he said the children appeared in reasonably good spirits and were active. They talked about the fact that they did have families but were only temporarily separated from them and verbalized feelings about their future. Several expressed anxieties accompanied by insomnia and other vague somatic complaints. The size of the group of unaccompanied children increased to eighteen at the time of Dr. Looney's second visit, and they were being housed in a quonset hut. This time Dr. Looney noted the prevailing mood was one of lethargy and hopelessness. Three children in particular manifested rather marked signs of depression. On this alarming note, Dr. Looney sent a memo to the commanding officer of Camp Pendleton dated June 18, 1975. These children, in contrast to the first visit only a week before, now felt they were different from other children in the camp, left out and alone. They no longer attempted to interact with other people in the camp, but lay in bed both day and night, with little or no sound sleep. No organized activities were available to them.

On his third visit to the unaccompanied children, Dr. Looney noted they had been moved to a larger building near the entrance to Camp 8. This time the number had increased from eighteen to forty. There were twelve girls with a mean age of 14.5 years and twenty-eight boys with a mean age of twelve years. Dr. Looney noted some very disturbing themes. Two girls and one boy were depressed enough to be suicidal. Other children and adolescents exhibited noticeable deterioration of their needs. They reported other children in Camp 8 made fun of them. They felt their third move had physically separated them from the rest of the refugees, and they consequently were stigmatized. The latter was in fact done when, at least for a short while, these children were asked to wear arm-bands for purposes of identification. In addition, they were taken to the head of the chow lines making hundreds of Vietnamese angry.

As a result, those with their *de facto* refugee foster families became more anxious and fearful they were not good enough to be taken out by the sponsors as a part of the family. The uncertainty often was expressed behaviorally rather than verbally. These children became hypersensitive and tended to take every gesture as a sign of rejection by their unofficial foster relatives and parents. Thus they were eventually identified and transferred to the unaccompanied children's quarters. In one communication, the consulting psychiatrist indicated his concern over the uneasiness of the Red Cross Volunteer Nurses with their responsibilities of managing the unaccompanied children's facilities. Even though these volunteer nurses were well trained and experienced, none had previous experience in dealing with a large number of distressed children and teen-agers.

At the end of the third and final consulting visitation with the unaccompanied children, Dr. Looney made several concrete recommendations to the medical authorities and to the military commander of the camp. These recommendations could be grouped into two categories. First, no further actions be permitted to separate unaccompanied childn from their unofficial foster homes. Second, find Vietnamese foster homes for the already separated unaccompanied children, either in camp with other refugees or outside the camp with non-refugee or resettled refugees.

As it turned out, these recommendations were not considered

by the civilian authorities of the refugee resettlement program in the camp. Physicians and psychiatrists from the Navy medical corps were frustrated by their inability to take immediate actions following Dr. Looney's recommendations. In August, upon confirming the news that the Interagency Task Force had contacted the Welfare Department of San Diego County to find foster homes for the unaccompanied children, a meeting was convened by some Asian American mental health professionals who had previously dealt with Asian children. Present at this meeting were one consulting psychiatrist from the Navy (who was asked to take charge of the care of the unaccompanied children in the camp), an executive of the County Welfare Department, a social worker of Asian descent from Los Angeles who had previously worked with children in group home situations, and several other Asian American mental health workers.

Two decisions were reached at this meeting. First, agreeing essentially with Dr. Looney's suggestions, the group felt the unaccompanied children should be cared for by Vietnamese families, regardless of whether these families had been sponsored out of the camp, but preferably in a group cottage cared for by Vietnamese couples who were seeking employment. Second, to implement the first suggestion, a meeting was to be arranged with the highest civilian authorities of the camp.

The meeting was held a week later. It was a short meeting. Arguments were presented from the viewpoint of psychiatric experts and some Asian American mental health workers. The final word was that the decision to place the unaccompanied children in regular homes through the efforts of the San Diego Welfare Department had already been made. The notion that whenever possible Asian homes be priority homes was mentioned but no assurance was made that this would indeed be the case. There were too few Asian homes in the San Diego area, and refugee families already had their share of problems in finding sponsors who were able and willing to accept very large refugee family groups.

Commenting on the entire situation, the group of medical personnel who played an important role in setting up the Crisis Center and in establishing a mental health clinic, stated:

"In our initial contacts we made, as seen in retrospect, a critical error. That is, we presumed the medical director had the

power to implement our medical suggestions. It turned out that State Department personnel actually had the power to negate many of our medical suggestions, such as our recommended adoption policies for unaccompanied children. We might have exerted greater consultor influence if we had correctly identified the sources of community power early in our involvement and tried dealing more directly with these persons."—Rahe, et al. 1976:13

In spite of these difficulties and renewed effort on the part of several psychiatric personnel to safeguard the mental health of the children from further deterioration, the combined effort of the Navy psychiatric team was perhaps the most important contribution in dealing with a serious but unpublicized and potentially explosive situation in Camp Pendleton. The establishment of a psychiatric crisis clinic was the most crucial decision made in dealing with the crisis situation and in monitoring the day-to-day conditions of the camp.

The unaccompanied children were slowly but surely placed by social workers of the County's Welfare Department, in some cases, against the psychiatric opinion in the camp. Several psychiatrists and social scientists discussed the possibilities of monitoring the unaccompanied children outside the camp. This plan was considered important from two perspectives. From the viewpoint of the attending psychiatrist assigned to take care of the children, the move to place some of the most disturbed children outside the camp was a way for the camp administration to avoid the responsibilities of probable breakdowns and suicides. The Navy psychiatrists felt it was their responsibility to see that these children be placed in the best possible environment so their condition would not deteriorate further. From the viewpoint of social scientists asked to monitor the mental health conditions, it would be interesting to find out if cross-cultural placement at this very early stage of cultural adjustment would speed up the process of Americanization—thus speaking positively of the program—or hinder the improvement of their already damaged mental states.

On November 21, 1975, a group of specialists gathered on the campus of the University of California, San Diego, to discuss what future actions could be taken to remedy the situation. Attending the meeting were two Navy psychiatrists who were assigned to take care of the mental health problems of the unaccompanied children, and a physician-psychiatrist who had a private practice and had been asked to see many refugee patients in the San Diego area. Two child psychologists of Asian heritage were also present at the meeting. One of the two child psychologists was on staff at the National Institute of Mental Health; the other was a researcher at the University of California, Davis campus. Also present were a sociologist who had just completed a study on child adoption, and a Vietnamese psychiatrist who had responsibilities in taking care of the unaccompanied children in the camp.

Several new pieces of information were revealed at this meeting. It was learned that the number of unaccompanied children being sent through the unaccompanied children's facilities was between seventy and one hundred during the time when the site was changed from Camps 1, 2, and 3 to Camp 8 and the time of the meeting in November. The capacity of the facilities was about thirty at any one time. There were five times more male children than female children and adolescents. Four major types of mental health problems were identified: anti-social behavior (rowdiness, minor rioting, tearing up compound); depression, withdrawal, and hysteria.

There were three types of unaccompanied children. The first category consisted of children who were at Camp Pendleton with relatives closer than cousins but not with parents, i.e., uncles or aunts. There were 208 such cases. The second category consisted of children who were at Camp Pendleton with relatives other than parents or uncles and aunts. The number was between thirty and forty. The third category consisted of children at Camp Pendleton who were completely unaccompanied. The figure was placed at between seventy to one hundred.

The psychiatrists were of the opinion that while the reasons for immigration of the children varied from accidental to conscious choice, it was important to note that the exercise of control in the selection process played an important part in subsequent dysfunctional behavioral manifestations. For example, it was expected that depression would be a more serious problem than in the children who had planned to evacuate. In evaluating the adjustment of the unaccompanied children to their foster parents, a critical factor to study would be the quantity of material goods provided.

At the end, the group decided to find systematic ways to follow up on the adjustment of these unaccompanied children. However, these plans eventually met strong resistance from administrators of the County Welfare Department which acted as the legal guardian of these children. Without the consent of the responsible personnel of the County, professional personnel were unable to reach these children for observation. Numerous efforts were made to find ways to monitor the adjustment of these children and they all failed.

8

The Sponsorship Program and Refugee Resettlement

Who ever said starting life over in a new country was going to be easy?—IATF official

Sponsorship out of camp to begin a "new life" was the next step for the Vietnamese refugee. This was a step not always taken enthusiastically, for whatever the disadvantages and unpleasantness of camp life, the camp gave a sense of security and met some of the basic physical needs. Even more it afforded the security of familiar people from the "Vietnamese village."

Closing the camps.—Journalists noted the development of "campitis" or a growing reluctance of refugees to leave the familiarity and security of the bases, in spite of the less than comfortable conditions of the camp. Many who had nothing but their clothes were concerned about the future management of the practical course of their lives.

A Vietnamese management consultant who had been in business with Americans commented that many refugees, especially the less sophisticated, were fearful. "They are very much afraid. They are very uncertain about the future. A lot of them are afraid to leave" (Kneeland, *New York Times*, July 22, 1975).

A great deal of concern was expressed about leaving other Vietnamese with whom they had regrouped in the camp and knew well enough to call companions in crisis. In extreme cases, "they keep hiding when you try to match them with a sponsor" *(New York Times*, July 22, 1975). And as N. G. W. Thorne, IATF Civilian Administrator at Camp Pendleton noted, "They realize when they pass out of this camp, this is the last bit of Vietnam they're going to see" *(New York Times*, July 22, 1975, p. 13).

Initially sponsorship was to be individual to encourage dispersal rather than concentration of the Vietnamese refugee population, a decision greeted with enthusiasm by those from states expecting to receive more than their share of refugees, as Congressman Mineta's staff report made clear (Mineta, *et al.*, 1975). Presumably, scattered settlement policy was considered desirable because it would avoid taxing the limited health and welfare resources of any one community; discourage the creation of a ghetto with long lasting housing, economic, and social consequences; and finally, lighten the burden on individual American families.

During the months of July and August, the Task Force, under strong Congressional pressure, decided to speed up the sponsorship program. As a result, all camps closed pretty much on schedule—Eglin Air Force Base, September 15; Guam, October 31; Camp Pendleton, October 31; Indiantown Gap, December 15; and Fort Chaffee, December 31, 1975. As of January 1, 1976, responsibilities for the Indo-China Refugee Resettlement Project passed from the Interagency Task Force to the Department of Health, Education and Welfare. Table 69 indicates the state of resettlement of the refugees. California received by far the most refugees with 27,199, but thirty-two other states received over 1,000 each.

Of 33,000 refugees surveyed, there was no bunching up at the end of hard-to-place refugees. For example, 2.13 percent had no formal education, but they did not dominate those still awaiting sponsorship. The survey showed that they made up one percent of those already released and 2.81 percent of those remaining in camp. The same general trend held for large families, the most glaring exceptions being the peasant classes of farmers and fishermen, who constituted only 1.68 percent of the total refugee population. Single men also were somewhat harder to place *(Washington Post*, September 14, 1975).

Donald MacDonald, Civilian Director of Camp Fort Chaffee, reported the voluntary resettlement agencies have said publicly "the Vietnamese represent the easiest group to resettle that we've encountered in the past thirty-nine years." He expected to wind up with only a few terminal cancer patients, a few old persons without family, and some emotionally and mentally retarded kids *(Washington Post*, September 14, 1975).

Table 69

NUMBER OF REFUGEES RESETTLED BY STATE

State	Total	State	Total
Alabama	1,262	New Hampshire	161
Alaska	81	New Jersey	1,515
Arkansas	2,042	New Mexico	1,040
Arizona	1,059	New York	3,806
California	27,199	North Carolina	1,261
Colorado	1,790	North Dakota	448
Connecticut	1,175	Ohio	2,924
Delaware	155	Oklahoma	3,689
District of Columbia	1,254	Oregon	2,063
Florida	5,322	Pennsylvania	7,159
Georgia	1,331	Rhode Island	223
Hawaii	2,039	South Carolina	759
Idaho	412	South Dakota	545
Illinois	3,696	Tennessee	922
Indiana	1,785	Texas	9,130
Iowa	2,593	Utah	559
Kansas	1,897	Vermont	150
Kentucky	967	Virginia	3,733
Louisiana	3,602	Washington	4,182
Maine	375	West Virginia	195
Maryland	2,319	Wisconsin	1,821
Massachusetts	1,169	Wyoming	115
Michigan	2,200	Guam	778
Minnesota	3,802	American Samoa	1
Mississippi	388	Puerto Rico	1
Missouri	2,699		
Montana	198	Unknown	6,500
Nebraska	1,211		
Nevada	338	Deaths	76
Total			128,186*

*Does not include 6,588 persons resettled in third countries.

Source: IATF, 1975a

On the other hand, in the *New York Times:*

"Whatever their evaluation of the program, even among those who feel it has been relatively successful, it is generally agreed that this resettlement has far outstripped in problems the absorption of the Cubans and Hungarians, the other large groups that have arrived in recent years."—New York Times, November 24, 1975

"Some critics complain that the resettlement has been too slow, forcing many refugees to remain for months in the military camps. Certainly it has taken far longer than the ninety days

envisioned by the Government. . . . Other critics complain that it has all happened too fast, that thousands of refugees, many of them unskilled, have been sent into a strange new world with little or no language training and with no attempt to train them for jobs that are scarce at best."—New York Times, November 24, 1975

Kunz indicated some pressure to end the "refugee problem" by resettling the refugees and considering the case closed. Despite the humanitarian concerns this country is noted for, to quickly get rid of the refugee problem and close the camp was too simplistic and "efficient" an operation. This rapid treatment of a serious problem exposed a less favorable side of the entire program. Forty-three percent of the 130,000 refugees were resettled in eleven weeks and 100 percent in nine months, compared with fourteen months for 40,000 Hungarians (Kneeland, *New York Times,* July 22, 1975).

Clearly then, there was a conflict between the camp time desired by at least some of the refugees and that desired by the host country. Transition from one stage to another was thus problematic and subject to competing definitions of urgency. Of course, the host country was able to mobilize social pressure by "counseling" the refugees. Unpleasant camp conditions and pressure to close the camp presumably ultimately forced the matter to an end. Refugees were drawn to the security and presence of other Vietnamese in the camp but were pressured to move from the uncomfortable physical conditions and lassitude of the camp, as well as, in many cases, drawn by a concern to secure good sponsors, jobs, and situations.

Organization and procedures of sponsorship.—Nine *Volags* (voluntary agencies) were contacted by the government to handle resettlement of the refugees in the United States. United HIAS (3,600 resettled, estimated final total number based on December 4, 1975 figures); Lutheran Immigration and Refugee Service (17,000); Tolstoy Foundation (3,300); International Rescue Committee (18,000); Church World Services (17,000); American Fund for Czechoslovak Refugees (818); United States Catholic Conference (48,000); Travelers Aid International Social Service (500), and Council for Nationalities Service (IATF 1975b, Annex, p. 25-26).

The nine resettlement agencies operated offices at each of the four refugee reception centers (except the American Fund for Czechoslovak Refugees, present at only two centers), with professional caseworkers assisted by volunteers and refugee translators. Local parishes or affiliates selected sponsors—individual families, congregations, other groups—and coordinated various forms of assistance from other volunteer groups.

In camp, each refugee selected a resettlement agency. If a refugee had no preference, the government assigned one. For refugees whose sponsors had specified them, the agency contacted the sponsor to determine ability to fulfill financial and moral responsibility. When refugee and sponsor agreed, the agency gave authorization to begin processing which took one to two weeks.

When the refugees had no specific sponsors—which was true in the majority of cases—volunteer agencies called on their national organizations. Case workers interviewed the refugees to determine family size, composition, job skills, and geographic preference and matched the family with an available sponsor. The time required for arrangements depended on the availability of sponsors and the refugees' vocational qualifications.

Sponsorship could include offers of support, employment, or both. Sponsors were individuals, churches, civic organizations, state and local government, or other organizations. Responsibilities of sponsors included (1) receiving the refugee and his family; (2) providing shelter and food until the refugee became self-sufficient (shelter need not necessarily be in the residence of the sponsor); (3) providing clothing and pocket money initially; (4) providing assistance in finding employment and helping with school registration for children; and (5) providing ordinary medical costs or medical insurance.

As time went on, pressure to resettle the refugees led to having large numbers of families sponsored rather than individual families. Group sponsorships provided more advantages because of the greater resources available and comprehensive services possible. Offers of group employment also were received by the Task Force.

A five hundred dollar grant per refugee was authorized to the Volag with considerable latitude in handling the money. Several agencies provided the refugee head of household a small amount of cash for each family member at the time of departure as well as a transitional allowance to be used at the point of resettlement. Others reserved a substantial portion of the money for follow-ups or continuations of services and support. All assisted refugees in finding housing, employment, educational placement, medical care, and miscellaneous services, such as legal advice, job workshops, Vietnamese language newspaper, etc.

Problems of the sponsorship program.—Various problems arose with sponsorship programs through the Volags, mostly because of the decision to let the Volags operate independently under the Task Force's assumption that "the Volags are the experts" and that "it never intended to tell the experts how to do what they do the best" (Mineta, *et al.* 1975:23).

Mineta points out that probably the most critical decision the refugee made was deciding which of the nine voluntary agencies would handle his/her resettlement in the United States. Yet the refugee was usually unaware that there was no uniform procedure among the agencies for processing and financial assistance. Each agency had its own definition of sponsorship and set its own criteria for acceptance or rejection.

One difference was evident to the refugee: the handling of the five hundred dollars per sponsored refugee reimbursed to the Volag. Specification for the use of the money was not made. According to Fernanto Oaxaca, Associate Director of the Office of Management and Budget, John McCarthy of the United States Catholic Conference said it was not "the policy of his voluntary agency to give any money directly to the refugees or their sponsors to help them in the resettlement process" (Mineta *et al.*, 1975, p. 24). The five hundred dollars was designed to help the refugee in resettlement; however, overhead costs of the Volag were deducted from this sum. The Volags were not required to account for allocation of the money to reserves for the future, even when current needs existed. Some of these agencies did not sign contracts:

"There exists no stipulation," conceded Robert Mott, the State Department's Executive Director for Humanitarian Affairs, "that agencies return any leftover funds, or interest earned on them, when the resettlement program expires in September, 1977. Nor is there real provision for the government to disallow agency expenditures it disagrees with."—Chicago Tribune, December, 1975

Table 70

ASSISTANCE RECEIVED FROM SPONSOR BY TYPES OF SPONSOR
(WEIGHTED PERCENTAGES)

Type of Sponsor	Un-weighted N	Assistance Received*								
		Financial	Food	Clothing	Transportation	Job Hunting	School Enrollment	English Class Enrollment	Other	None Received
Total . . .	1,551	22.7	64.7	59.3	48.4	64.0	22.4	21.4	4.6	14.1
Individual	250	21.8	54.3	46.8	39.1	46.8	13.9	12.7	4.4	23.9
Family . .	872	21.8	67.4	60.1	52.8	54.6	20.5	22.8	3.8	14.6
Group . .	429	26.5	69.0	70.7	45.6	61.5	36.3	26.0	7.0	7.9

For many of the agencies, the bulk of the refugees' expenses were borne by church and individual sponsors as was the task of finding jobs and housing. Millions of dollars voted by the Congress for resettlement which could have been mobilized for current refugee programs were scheduled to be kept as "contingency funds for future refugee needs."

Some specifics: (1) Lutheran Immigration and Refugee Service to receive $7,850,000 for 15,700 refugees; plans to spend $2 million in 1975, and as of October 31, 1975 had outlaid 82.7 percent of this for administrative and other expenses and only 17.3 percent toward the refugees; officials expect this ratio to change in the future. (2) United States Catholic Conference to receive $23,731,000 and plans to spend $300 on actual resettlement per head and $130 per refugee allotment for administrative costs. $3.3 million would be left in reserve (cf. *Chicago Tribune*, Jeff Lyon, December, 1975).

In practice the Volags gave the refugees ten dollars per person in travel money. Some refugees did leave with additional financial resources, depending on the agency. Refugees resettled under similar circumstances but by different Volags may have received different sums of transition funds on leaving the camp, a non-uniformity apparent to the refugees afterwards, if not at that time. (See Table 71.)

Some points made by Congressman Mineta and staff about the Volags:

(1) Lack of accountability of the Volags to the Task Force which intentionally did not monitor the Volags;

(2) Volags did not tabulate actual cost of resettlement—estimated by Church World Services to be less than five hundred dollars. Mineta asked whether the same expenditure was incurred for individuals in whole families as for individuals alone;

(3) Volags were contracted to maintain individual records of location, employment status, and education of each refugee for only thirty days after resettlement. It is difficult to have good management without information on performance and follow-up. And independent evaluation is impossible;

(4) In many cases, Volags were negligent in following up refugees, thus overlooking problems.

"According to one Volag representative at Indiantown Gap, the only Volag contact with the sponsored refugee or family comes

Table 71

VOLAG SPENDING ON REFUGEES

V O L A G	A AVERAGE COST PER REFUGEE	B TRANSITION MONEY	C TRAVELING MONEY	D MONEY OUT OF THE $500 GOING TO LOCAL OFFICES	E MONEY OUT OF THE $500 GOING TO NAT'L OFFICES
U.S. CATHOLIC CONFERENCE	1000.00	NONE	10.00	330.00	170.00
CHURCH WORLD SERVICES	?	100.00	10.00	?	?
LUTHERAN IMMIGRATION AND REFUGEE SERVICE	1350.00	NONE	10.00	—	500.00
TOLSTOY FOUNDATION	?	NONE	10.00	—	500.00
AMERICAN COUNCIL FOR NAT' LITTIES SERVICES	?	NONE	10.00	400.00	100.00
TRAVELERS' AID	?	NONE	10.00	400.00	100.00
AMER. FUND FOR CZECHOSLOVAK REFUGEES	?	NONE	10.00	—	500.00
UNITED HIAS	?	100.00	10.00	450.00	50.00
INTERNATIONAL RESCUE COMMITTEE	2100.00	NONE	10.00	?	?

Source: Mineta, 1975

approximately three to four weeks after the refugee leaves the camp. However, the staff person did maintain that the refugee does know where he/she can contact his/her voluntary agency should any need arise."—Mineta, *et al.*, 1975:27

(5) Failure to maintain records resulted in failure to cope with sponsorship breakdown and necessitated refugees going on welfare. Volags were required to file quarterly reports on number of sponsorship breakdowns. However, in some cases, the only way a sponsorship breakdown was detected by a Volag was when they happened to see a particular refugee on a state welfare roll.

Success of the sponsorship program.—Mineta referred to the sponsor/refugee relationship as fragile, basing this statement on newspaper reports. Information on sponsorship breakdown is difficult to verify. In Los Angeles, Catholic Relief Service was quoted as declaring a total of seven-hundred breakdowns among families handled by that agency alone. Officials of the Interagency Task Force reported breakdowns at only about two percent, but the *New York Times* suggested that it ran higher: "It depends on how you define it," said Mr. Sternberg of the International Rescue Committee, meaning that movements to a new sponsor or location are not the same as catastrophic breakdown. Mrs. Julia Taft, head of the Interagency Task Force for Indo-Chinese refugees, declared, "You're dealing with 130,000 personalities. Sometimes it's the refugees, sometimes it's the sponsor; but whatever it is, it's still a very insignificant number" (*New York Times*, November 24, 1975).

William Richards, the West Coast Bureau Chief of the *Washington Post*, after exhaustive investigations of the whole resettlement program, said in desperation that the scattered resettlement did not work. Large streams of Vietnamese refugees gravitated toward metropolitan centers where they had friends and relatives, and where they occasionally could enjoy cultural facilities such as an Asian restaurant or bookstore. Many hotels and public institutions in San Diego and Los Angeles were known for frequent gatherings of refugees for social purposes as well as for the exchange of information regarding employment opportunities, health and welfare resources, and other helping facilities. The extent of such needs and available resources remained largely unknown to the refugees themselves and to social and welfare agencies.

A news story in the *Washington Post* mentioned such horrors as the use of refugees as house servants, forced participation in homosexual acts, and flight of refugees back to the camp where they were turned away for fear of alarming remaining unsponsored refugees. The government, according to the news report, set up breakdown centers in Houston and Miami. Halleck Rose, Director of the International Rescue Center, talked of problems which in some cases were the fault of the refugees and in others, the mistakes of American families. Rose said the government was spending more than $1,000 a month in hotel and food bills for each refugee family. His office also was giving $80 to each adult and $20 to each child. Rose said refugees who broke from their sponsors came from as far away as Nebraska and Tennessee, and most refugees who returned wanted to stay in California because of its imported Asian food and its warm climate.

The shift from individual to group sponsorship helped the pace of resettlement: Mark Ice, head of the Lutheran Immigration and Refugee Services said: "Of our breakdowns—and we've had very few—nearly all have been individual sponsors." Group sponsorships were emphasized from the beginning:

"You have more people, a broader financial base. You don't tend to run into the problems of a personality clash . . . They get a very good feeling that there are a lot of people concerned about them."—Washington Post, September 14, 1975

The First Wave Report in October by the Interagency Task Force provided some firsthand data, in spite of the considerable problem of obtaining location and phone numbers of the refugees. Out of a random sample of 1,570, the majority of refugees (80 percent) said they were satisfied with the sponsorship. Of the remaining 20 percent who expressed dissatisfaction, one third experienced complete dissatisfaction. Of these "not at all" satisfied, reasons given were: sponsor looks down on us (78.9 percent); sponsor treats us like servants (66.9 percent); and sponsor does not give us help as originally promised (63.4 percent); some reported difficulty in communicating needs (31.2 percent); language barrier (22.4 percent); and incompatible ways of life (16.0 percent).

For the "somewhat dissatisfied," the problems of communication, language barrier, and far different ways of life were more significant (89.9 percent, 77.6 percent, 85.0 percent respectively), but less difficulty existed in general treatment and help from sponsor (IATF 1975a, pp. 17-18).

In this survey, 60 percent of the refugees reported they were not receiving any type of federal assistance. Only 20 percent of the families were receiving food stamps, and 16 percent of the refugees were receiving financial assistance.

There was a slight tendency for families who had been out of camp longer to receive assistance, perhaps because of learning about assistance programs after a time lag.

The year end report (December 1, 1975) of the Department of Health, Education and Welfare listed a larger number of refugees on welfare than what the public was led to believe. The figure was something like one out of every five families.

Representative McClory of Illinois called the rise in refugee welfare recipients "disturbing and frightening" *(Chicago Tribune*, December, 1975). The *Chicago Tribune* pointed out that contingency funds still were being held by the Volags for a rainy day and that day seems to have come. The Volags justified reserve funds by pointing out that they (1) have met legitimate needs, (2) have vocational and other long-term programs planned, (3) have extensive follow-up, and (4) are expecting future breakdowns for which they must provide.

Still the *Tribune* suggested that going on welfare was already a breakdown, one to be handled with these funds. There was the suggestion that once on welfare, the Indo-Chinese refugee with his lack of language skills was likely to get bogged down.

R. Friedman, HEW Regional Director, questioned the assumption that it would be difficult to make the refugees self-sufficient. Mrs. Taft, on the other hand, stated that there is no problem with refugees having both service programs and financial assistance, that large numbers of the Vietnamese were expected to go on welfare, and that self-sufficiency was only a long-term goal *(Chicago Tribune*, December 1975). Both, in different ways, were denying that there was a problem of refugees going on welfare. Admitting there was such a problem implied failure of the program or the need for further effort.

There were some differences among the Volags in terms of families receiving federal assistance. (See Table 72.) The highest percentage of families *not* receiving federal assistance was 77.0 percent and the lowest 52 percent; more families received food stamps than any other form of assistance. There was little difference by type of sponsor; however, a lower proportion of "no sponsor" families received Federal assistance than "sponsored" families.

Regarding sponsor assistance: in general, a higher proportion of refugee families under group sponsorship received assistance from their sponsor than refugee families under individual or family sponsorship. This was true regardless of types of assistance with the exception of transportation.

There is no information in the First Wave Report of breakdown in sponsorship. But sponsorship breakdown was in direct proportion to time elapsed. In the first few months after these camps were closed, several attempts were made to estimate the extent to which sponsorship broke down, but the exact figure is unknown.

Employment, housing, and income.—Jobs proved to be a major problem in resettling the refugees. The official report from time to time estimated the unemployment rate as high as 50 percent despite the generally selectively superior status of the refugee population with respect to education and previous occupation.

As of the First Wave Report, October 2, 1975, the employment rate for persons over fourteen years was 68.2 percent for males and 50.9 percent for females. The data showed a substantially higher percentage of household members other than the head currently working and contributing to the support of the family group. The most notable exception being "female parents." (See IATF, 1975a, Table 2.)

Slightly more than one-third of all persons fourteen years or older were unemployed (persons who want to work, who are out of work and currently looking for a job). Other data suggested working refugees were significantly *underemployed*. In the First Wave Report, the majority of heads of households had been in professional, managerial/technical, sales, and clerical positions in Vietnam; however, they didn't appear to be doing as well as the blue collar worker (except for craftsmen) in their employment role (IATF, 1975a, Table 9). "When the present occupation of the household heads is compared to their Vietnamese occupation and by proficiency in English, the majority of them are found to be underemployed. Only 19.5 percent are employed at comparable

Table 72

TYPES OF FEDERAL ASSISTANCE BY VOLAG
(WEIGHTED PERCENTAGES)

VOLAG	Unweighted N	None Received	Assistance Received				
			Food Stamps	Medical Aid	Refugee Financial Assistance	SSI	Other
Total	1,570	60.4	21.4	17.9	18.2	.5	24.0
American Fund for Czchoslovak Refugees	10	52.0	20.0	4.0	-	-	.9
American World Service	176	62.6	20.4	15.4	16.4	1.3	1.3
International Rescue Committee	273	50.8	27.7	20.2	27.1	.4	.8
Immigration and Refugee Service	259	63.1	24.2	16.7	13.1	.3	-
Foundation.	37	77.0	17.6	14.9	6.8	-	-
Visited Hias Service	61	64.9	27.2	10.5	10.5	1.8	1.9
S.C.C.	549	60.5	18.3	19.6	20.2	.4	-
Other	114	67.3	14.9	13.0	13.0	-	
VOLAG	94	64.1	21.5	19.5	11.8	1.5	4.1

occupational levels and 4.5 percent at a higher level" (IATF, 1975a, pp. 12-13, see also Table 14, IATF, 1975a, Table 10).

Some factors which may have affected the employment rate:

1) Length of time since departure from camp.

2) Agency. Persons processed out by Lutheran Immigration and Refugee Service or United HIAS had better employment rates.

3) Age. Highest employment rate for males is between 25-44; little difference for females in the range 14-44. Males in the oldest group (over 55) seem to have most difficulty—so do females in this age range, but there are fewer of them.

4) Education. There is no tendency for the more highly educated Vietnamese to be the most successful in finding employment; however, the groups with no formal degrees are the least successful.

Table 73

EMPLOYMENT STATUS OF HEADS OF HOUSEHOLD
BY VIETNAM OCCUPATION
(WEIGHTED PERCENTAGES)

Vietnam Occupation	Unweighted	Employed	Unemployed
Total	1,262	65.4	34.6
Professional	389	68.3	31.7
Managers	423	67.6	32.4
Sales	23	50.0	50.0
Clerical	230	63.4	36.6
Craftsmen	98	62.6	37.4
Operative	11	91.8	8.2
Transport	16	85.7	14.3
Laborers	41	72.1	27.9
Other Services	16	80.0	-
Farmers	5	-	-
Farm Laborers	1	-	

5) English proficiency. The rate of employment is associated with English proficiency, and a high proportion of people who are not in the labor force are those who do not know English at all (IATF, 1975a, pp. 10-12).

Heads of households responded to questions about job-hunting methods; help from the sponsor and American friends was most useful. Problems in obtaining jobs were "overqualification," "no vacancy," and "lack of English proficiency" (IATF, 1975a, Table 16).

Data on income shows 42.0 percent of the refugee households surveyed had an income between $2,500 and $4,999, and only 2 percent had an income over $10,000. Length of time since departure from camp did not seem related to the income situation of the family (IATF, 1975a, Table 17 and p. 15).

The job and income situation of the refugees thus looked somewhat bleak for the refugees in October, based on hard data rather than journalistic impressions, even though sponsorship per se seemed to be working out relatively well.

Housing at this time was also perhaps less than desirable, as approximately half of all refugee families resided in the home of their sponsors; 36.5 percent lived in rented quarters of their own. The higher the income, the more likely the family was to have its own housing (IATF, 1975a, p. 18).

It seems likely in this sample, given the relatively large number of "other relatives" living in the household, that the high rate of labor force participation suggested more than one (nuclear) family group living in a number of refugee households (IATF, 1975a, pp. 8-9).

A grim picture of the situation in Chicago and vicinity as of the end of September was portrayed in the *Milwaukee Journal:*

"Many of the 300 Vietnamese refugees now living on the North Side are housed in high crime areas, have menial jobs or are unemployed and cannot locate apartments for their often large-sized families . . . The refugees, most of them recently arrived from Fort Chafee, Arkansas, are generally ill-clothed for the cooler Illinois climate and are in dire need of winter clothing."—Milwaukee Journal, Sept. 28, 1975

Liese Lee Haag, an official of Jewish Family and Community Services, said:

"Jobs are scarce, apartments difficult to find, and money for skill training programs unavailable.

"We're hustling and the Vietnamese are hustling," she explained. *"We have 80 volunteers walking the streets looking for apartments. Sometimes there are six to ten in a family. How do you find an apartment for a man earning $110 to $120 a week?*
. . .

"Haag said the Vietnamese, mostly from middle class backgrounds, now lacked the comforts they were used to. She said their apartments were often substandard, the neighborhood

unsafe, and work either not available or difficult to handle. Many of the men, for example, had applied for day labor jobs but could not handle them because of their slim physiques.

"*Haag criticized the Department of HEW for virtually abandoning the Vietnamese refugees in Chicago.*"—Milwaukee Journal, Sept. 28, 1975

Haag maintained the $500 subsidy was insufficient in a northern climate. Similar problems were being reported by Travelers Aid in Chicago although Catholic Charities refugees were having a somewhat easier employment time—if they spoke English (*Milwaukee Journal*, Sept. 28, 1975).

Confronted with the criticism of HEW, Hiroshi Kanno, assistant to HEW administrator Richard Friedman, said his agency was aware of the problems of the newly relocated Vietnamese, but "We're not structured to do a 'laying on hands' kind of servicing . . . We have to rely on state and local agencies" (*Milwaukee Journal*, Sept. 28, 1975). The *Journal* editorialized, "It is a tragedy that private agencies, with only minimal government subsidies, should be told to carry the ball in acclimating the Vietnamese to the American way of life" (*Milwaukee Journal*, Sept. 28, 1975).

Yet the comment of Mrs. Taft that "No one guaranteed anybody a chicken in every pot" (*Chicago Tribune*, December, 1975), suggests the view of the resettlement bureaucracy that the refugees were more or less responsible for themselves after the initial resettlement.

Overall refugee adjustment.—Again, we had two views. The official reports of some considerable accomplishment, i.e., 68 percent employment, all refugees resettled—and the reports of refugees who were in a depression-producing situation in which they had given up their homeland, familial ties, and economic security out of necessity for personal safety. They were in deprived circumstances, certainly relatively but also in terms of real need. They had not yet integrated into American society or developed a Vietnamese subcommunity.

There were many obstacles to readjustment. Refugees were frustrated because they could not obtain federal employment or enlist in the military. Refugees did not have the advantages of permanent resident alien status. Persons with careers or security built up in Vietnam had to start over, often with no hope of success, as former Navy Captain Nguyen Kim Huong Giang, who spent twenty-three years in the Vietnamese military but has "no specialty except leadership." A former customs agent, Nguyen Tri Hau, is more hopeful:

> *"I am a patient man; if I have to start over again, I believe I will make it someday. I believe I will become self-sufficient as an auto mechanic. Most refugees have only one hope: to have a job and become a tax payer."*—San Diego Union, May 2, 1976

To maintain such perseverance in the face of unemployment, under-employment, and low pay was not easy—or universal. The social and cultural losses were even harder to replace. After one year in America, refugees still had difficulty accepting American values such as (1) dispersal of the extended family, (2) numerical limits on home occupancy, (3) indifference and disrespect toward old people, (4) absence of friendly people with whom to socialize in the daytime, (5) hectic pace with few breaks in the work day, (6) distances which require vehicular transportation rather than including work, family, and sociability in a confined, easily accessible geographic area, (7) value on work and achievement rather than interpersonal ties (Interviews in the *San Diego Union*, May 1, 1976).

The Vietnamese came from a *gemeinschaft* social milieu, even though in an urban setting, with its strong ties of kinship and neighborhood. They came to a *gesellschaft* setting, a more impersonal society in which they were strangers and only to a limited extent could replace the work, family, friendship, and social network which had been ruptured, and enjoy the familiar events and customs.

9
Conclusion

*"Whether or not we will be happy in America de-
pends on you. We know that we were not welcomed
guests. If the people are nice, we will be happy."*—
female refugee

In spite of the material and mental health stresses of the Vietnamese refugees, little further assistance in terms of service and
training programs or in mental health services was anticipated.
Donald Wortman, then in charge of the resettlement program for
HEW, frankly admitted this, blaming the confusion of conflicting
statistics on the sponsorship problems and the limited budget at
his disposal, much of which ($100 million) was already obligated
to the voluntary agencies. In addition, the Ford administration
was fearful that the original stance the White House took in
dealing with New York City's financial problem might not be
consistent with policy in dealing with the refugee problem, particularly if additional funds were pumped into local and state
treasuries for the refugee resettlement programs. Also militat-
ing against further assistance was the romantic notion played up
by local newspapers—human interest stories about persons such
as a former high military commander in the South Vietnamese
armed forces who had found a new career, somewhat lower in
prestige, in a small community in Kansas living with his family
happily ever after. While these articles may have told of only a
few success stories, they were easily accepted due to the traditional American belief that newcomers are able to help themselves by working hard. No distinction was made between the
refugee and the voluntary migrant, the former with no preparation, resources, or cultural skills, but with the depression-

generating psychological ambivalence discussed earlier. Not only was practical help lacking, but *"One must also concede that not much attention had been given to and not as much was accomplished in the domain of mental health as in the field of material comfort for the refugees. One may find, here and there, mention of the culture shock, of the problems of adjusting to American society, but the measures taken so far seldom have been conceived as elements of an integrated program or part of a continuous effort to alleviate suffering and to prevent problems, the cost of which, otherwise, will be extremely high to the nation and to the individuals concerned."*—Tung, 1975b:11

Objections to this policy were heard, from persons such as Dale Dehaan, staff director to Senator Edward M. Kennedy's subcommittee on refugees, a part of the Senate Judiciary Committee.

"I think going down the pike there are going to be a lot of problems . . . Once the refugees were out of the camps the Task Force did not get involved in resettlement, depending on the voluntary agencies. I disagree with that. The basic supports have to come out of the government. There are certain things that are not going to be done for these refugees which have been done for other refugees because of the social policies of the administration."—New York Times, Nov. 24, 1975

The Vietnamese arrived as refugees in the U.S. at a time when

1) The public wanted to forget about Vietnam, hence they were not receptive to the reminder posed by Vietnamese refugees;

2) There was lingering prejudice against non-Caucasians;

3) The job situation was unpromising;

4) Interest was receding from social concerns and social action efforts, and persons and communities were thinking of their own economic welfare and sufficiencies.

In the resettlement, government bureaucracies were operating in their customary fashion. This resulted in some unfortunate characteristics of the program:

1) Few Asian-Americans or refugee Vietnamese included in planning or operation, hence little sensitivity to cultural shock and facilitation of intercultural adjustment;

2) Assumption of an assimilation strategy to meet the needs and goals of the refugees;

3) Dispersal of the refugees due to (a) assimilation strategy, and (b) desire to distribute the financial and service burden of the refugees, hence little opportunity for Vietnamese to obtain the social and psychological support of Vietnamese sub-communities which would have made psychological adjustment and mutual aid easier;

4) Pressure to resettle the refugees as rapidly as possible, however unsuitably or psychologically unprepared they were, in order to place refugees in the category of "voluntary migrants" who can take care of themselves and "make it" on their own in America;

5) Insufficient financial input and insufficient services, particularly after leaving the camp;

6) Insensitivity to mental health problems and needs in transit, in camp, and in resettlement; these less tangible problems of the refugee received very little attention compared with the more material ones;

7) Little concern for maintenance of the Vietnamese extended family or (in the case of unaccompanied children) of pseudo-familial relationships. In some cases immigration laws or resettlement arrangements required break-up of familial ties, especially at first—more sensitivity to this was developed later. This, as well as the perhaps rigid insistence on maintaining billeting assignments in the camps in opposition to natural movements and clusterings, showed an unawareness of the social fabric and its importance in ultimate readjustment;

8) The American privatized political system which permitted the federal government to delegate the resettlement task to disparate private agencies who operated in a non-uniform manner, causing (a) confusion and feelings of bad treatment on the part of refugees whose experiences and assistance were not comparable to those of their fellow refugees; and (b) lack of coordination resulting in some concern about possible misuse of money by Volags on the one hand, and feelings by the Volags that financial and service support by the government was insufficient on the other. Further delegation by the private agencies to local affiliates, who in turn coordinated private organizational and individual efforts, resulted, on the one hand, in the outpouring of voluntary activity and contributions for which this country was deservedly complimented, but, on the other, in the possibility for

insufficiency or even unpleasantness on the part of unsupervised individuals.

9) It also seemed impossible for bureaucracies to come up with imaginative programs for dealing with the intangible psychological aspects of resettlement, for by their very nature bureaucracies deal with routinized problems not involving emotions, feelings, and psychological problems.

Factors in the Vietnamese refugee situation which facilitated ultimately successful resettlement:

1) A relatively young, well-educated, skilled, and urban group of people;

2) A strong historic culture with values which encouraged discipline, accepting adversity with courage and stoicism; and a strong religious commitment which mitigated against antisocial behavior and discouragement;

3) Very strong extended-family ties which had practical advantages, i.e., many workers in one family as well as emotional support and integrative functions—older people and teen-agers, for example, could be given meaningful tasks, and the mature adults gained a feeling of value and responsibility;

4) Arrival at a time of interest in ethnicity and positive value of ethnic communities, as well as particular consciousness of Asians as a minority group, which would dispose persons to some awareness of prejudice and lack of opportunity;

5) Some previous exposure to American customs, work, and food, at least on the part of persons associated with American private and governmental organizations in Vietnam;

6) A very large proportion of young people who should have found adjustment easiest, particularly given the uniformity and "American" character of teenage culture around the world.

To summarize at a more abstract level, in Kunz's theoretical discussion of refugee problems, his sensitizing concepts are well-realized in the concrete particulars of the Vietnamese exodus and resettlement. The "acute" refugee flight characterized by a kinetic model in which "push" rather than "pull" is emphasized; the demographic characteristics of the refugee population predictable from Kunz's model, with the departure from ideal type, represented by the escape of Vietnamese family groups; the "midway to nowhere" malaise of the transit and camp; the bureaucratic pressures to declare the refugees resettled and equivalent to voluntary migrants, hence no longer a "problem"—all these are seen here. To the extent that the study of the Vietnamese refugees can illustrate Kunz's abstractions and add its own distinctive features—the aforementioned extended family; the anomaly of Asians in a Caucasian country; the private rather than governmental solution to social problems typical of this country—our knowledge is increased.

In considering the social psychology of the "process of becoming a refugee," there is a constant conflict over the definition of the situation and of the status of the refugee on the part of refugees and their spokesmen and the host society's bureaucrats, news media, and representatives of private organizations. This conflict over status continues in the observable stages of the refugee career.

Initially, at the time of flight, entry into the refugee status in an acute situation is not voluntary and the refugee is acted upon by the push of fear for personal safety during a political crisis—in this case, the fall of the Vietnamese regime. Plans are nonexistent and destination uncertain. Numerical and categorical limitations were placed on the refugees in their host countries. Because of chaos of the refugee flight, some refugees were able to escape these limitations, and the host country permitted the evasion to stand by accepting the refugees.

A broader problem for our country to consider is the political question of whether a greater effort should have been made to facilitate the frightened Vietnamese into becoming refugees, or whether refugees should have been discouraged on the grounds that their flight was really unnecessary and would result in a more difficult life than remaining in Vietnam.

During the second stage, refugees often did not know where they were bound by plane or ship. After arriving at a "midway to nowhere" point, they became the focus of pressures to return, to stay, or to continue, which also can be considered psychologically (double-bind, depression) as well as sociologically ("kinetics").

The third stage, the refugee camp, could be considered a social institution in itself, a "small city" or "Vietnamese village" to which the refugee had to adjust and be socialized—and to which some adjusted too well, becoming the victims of "campitis." Administrators and refugees and their spokesmen struggled over the timing of leaving camp and entry into the sponsorship stage.

The next stage—*sponsorship out*—was a hard adjustment. At this point, the basic definition of the Vietnamese as refugees (needing help) or voluntary migrants ("life in a new country is always hard"), as well as the rapidity with which the refugee was to make the transition to this stage, were much debated. In resettlement as well as in camp, the gap between the massive effort of the authorities and the needs of the refugees resulted in feelings that the other was inadequate. The government was in a more powerful position, so its definition prevailed. Earlier, at the time of escape, the sheer mass of people overwhelmed the government's resistance to extensive refugee flight, hence, to some extent, the refugees had the last word.

The continuity of this constant conflict and negotiation over the status and needs of the refugee and the definition of the situation was observed in the press, official reports, statistics, and public statements. The outcome fits Kunz's theoretical analysis in which the refugee is to be processed off the rolls as soon as possible, to merge with voluntary migrants and eventually with the general population. This is the definition of the situation toward which the host country and its attendant bureaucracy tend to strive; they clearly did so in this case.

Kunz's kinetic model of refugees' movements and destination implies the refugee was a passive reactor to these pressures and hence was placed where the government bureaucracy designated. The refugees and their spokesmen were not quite this passive. Lacking in resources of communication and media facilities, lacking in political power, lacking internal organization, and lacking facility in the new culture, they were not likely to be successful in a struggle with the receiving society for redefinition of the situation. They attempted to negotiate prolonged refugee status with accompanying provision of assistance, guidance, and services. Only individual refugees who resisted through evasion were likely to depart from the trajectory laid out for them, and in the process they probably were renouncing government assistance. Efforts of refugee advocates to force development of programs of financial services and sensitivity to mental health needs, taking as their point of departure the needs, desires, and preferences and problems of the refugee, did not seem to be successful. There was conflict and negotiation, but of unequal adversaries. The refugee, if he is to be successful, must be the recipient of or enlist the sympathy and assistance of other powerful figures (political, media) in the host society in securing the passage of the appropriated funds. Liaison figures (like Dr. Tung) in the refugee group who have the cultural understanding of both countries, the organizational talent and sophistication, and the articulateness to communicate needs are few in number. And, again, they are not powerful because they are aliens without a secure status in the host society or a position of power.

Conceptualization of the refugee problem in terms of 1) career stages; 2) perspectives, interests, and vantage points of the refugee and the host country on the same events; 3) conflict and negotiation of the definition of the situation, and entry and exit from refugee status, as well as 4) further use of Kunz's very well developed kinetic model of flight—all of this seems in order in the study of the Vietnamese refugee movement, as well as other refugee movements.

To return to the concrete problem of the Vietnamese refugees and their future, the problem of the Vietnamese refugees is not over, but the flow of refugees as a national problem now lies dormant. Because the refugee status arose from political-military decisions and events, not from the individual decisions and desires of the individuals involved for an envisioned better life or the natural social development of the group of people, the solution to some of these problems must be political in the sense of societal action through the political action and resources of the government. It must not be left to individual efforts or the unattended play of socio-economic forces, neither of which will compensate for the relative disadvantage of the Vietnamese in the economic struggle or the psychological difficulties which they can be expected to suffer. As Kunz has said, bureaucrats will suggest that there are no more problems of refugees and whatever problems which now surface must be thought of as normal problems of immigrants. This is only an easy way out. The burden of services must be shouldered by the federal, state, and local governments as well as by voluntary organizations. This report merely attempts to delineate the background, the events, and the social processes through which a segment of the Vietnamese population has become an American refugee problem.

As was stated by a Congressional staff member, "We haven't heard the last of the Vietnamese refugees" (*New York Times*, Nov. 24, 1975).

Appendix

Sampling Design
Interviewer Training
Interviewing Procedure

Sampling design.—With the continuous discharge of refugees from the camp as sponsors made their contacts and concluded arrangements with voluntary agencies, new waves of refugees poured in on a daily basis to fill the vacated spaces. To sample such a mobile population was like sampling the continuous flow of water in a river. Since it was important to sample the population according to the time of arrival and the varying lengths of stay in the camp, the decision was made to select random numbers each week, using one week as the time frame for the sampling procedure.

Random selection was done on an individual basis—according to the individual ID number given at the time of admission to the camp. Once an individual was selected, all members with an identical family ID were included as a sample unit. This method allowed the investigators to choose complete families, incomplete families with only related kin, or even single individuals without relatives. The original plan called for continuous sampling on a weekly basis until a total of fifty complete families were interviewed. The possibility existed to add an additional twenty to thirty incomplete families and an equal number of single individuals identified by random numbers.

There were four types of family units. The first type consisted of both parents and at least one child. The complete family unit, as it was later labelled, consisted of the parent-offspring relations and possibly, but not necessarily, other relatives. The second type unit consisted of one parent and offsprings, with or without relatives. (The single parent family later was merged with the complete family to form the basic data pool of family units.) The third group consisted of any related kin, such as siblings, married couple with no offsprings, grandparent(s) and grandchild(ren), or cousins, uncle-nephew relations, etc. And finally, the single individuals.

The sampling procedure had to be modified when the computer broke down. Upon such occasions, random numbers generated from the local telephone directory were used. Perhaps the most troublesome field situation, one which was not foreseen by the field workers, was the time lag in obtaining computer lists of individuals still in the camp. Computer listings generated from registration forms had to be card-punched before they were merged with the data tape. The process of transposing individual forms onto magnetic tape lagged behind the speed refugees were sponsored out of the camp during the months of August and September. For this reason, field workers found that computer lists became obsolete faster than current information became available. The failure of the computer system during the months of June, July, August, and September created even greater delays in processing all job requests.

As it turned out, a second type of computer listing became available toward the end of August. This was a master list of all refugees admitted to the camp between June 15 and August 19, 1975. All individuals were arranged alphabetically under the day of arrival. With this list, it was possible for research aides to search manually and to match family members who may have been admitted at different camp areas on different days. The matching by last name and other pertinent familial information was a tedious but significant job, for it put together more complete family groups than were known to the camp authorities.

Interviewer training and field situation.—After all instruments were prepared for the project, recruitment of interviewers began from among Vietnamese college and graduate students in the San Diego area.

Interviewer recruitment was done by individual interviews with applicants, assessing their verbal skills and their attitudes toward the work involved. Ten interviewers were selected with four additional names on the reserve list. A two day orientation session was conducted with all interviewers working collectively and individually with members of the training team and professional staff. Each question on the survey instrument was discussed, rehearsed, and used for training. All such sessions were tape recorded and used later with interviewers present to discuss alternative strategies. One psychiatrist took special pains to instruct interviewers on what to do if the respondent became overwhelmed by emotion during the interview session.

For the next two weeks, the research team worked around the clock to improve the wording of the instrument, pretesting it in the community with recently discharged Vietnamese families and conducting review sessions. Such preparations were so carefully made that even the sex, age, and social class of the interviewers were matched as closely as possible with the refugee-respondents in order to avoid any possible contamination due to differences in social background between the interviewer and the respondent.

The entire packet of interview schedule, questionnaires, and psychological scales were translated by a group of Vietnamese volunteers at a nearby university who had organized themselves and worked around the clock in shifts during the two week period prior to the camp interview. Questions that offended or violated Vietnamese sensibilities were reworded; inappropriate procedures were reviewed by the specialists to be changed and improved. When all of these reviews and improvements were made, the English version was again translated into Vietnamese, and the translated version screened for readability and clarity by a group of independent Vietnamese volunteers. After this final screening, the instrument was translated by an independent translator back into the English language. This English version of re-translation was compared to the original English version to determine what, if any, discrepancies had occurred during the translations which might alter the intent of the question. Different individuals were involved in each phase of the translation, and the original version was not given to the second translator.

The final Vietnamese version was pretested once more with a group of refugees located in San Diego. The pretesting was necessary to determine problems of introduction, instruction, and the length of time needed to conduct the entire interview. Special attention was paid to the sequence of the instruments so respondents would not be burdened with boring tasks for too long.

Interview procedure.—The day prior to the interview, a person selected by the predetermined random selection process was contacted by one of the interviewers. That person was then asked to identify the head of the household. A brief introduction was made to explain the nature of the interview and the medical examination. He was told one of the interviewers would return the next morning to accompany the family to the dispensary where the interview and medical examination would take place. During all contacts with the family, they were told they could refuse to answer any one question or the entire questionnaire and could terminate the interview at any time.

At the dispensary, the family was introduced to the Vietnamese interviewers, and the project was explained in greater detail. If they agreed, the entire family was divided into interview groups and each one separately interviewed. Between 11:00 A.M. and 1:00 P.M., depending upon the size of the family (hence the interview time required), each member of the family was given a physical examination. Arrangements were made for the family to have lunch after the physical examination across from the dispensary, instead of walking all the way back to their tent area to wait in line.

Obtaining data from members of the family was, in many ways, a cooperation between interviewers and family members as well as a division of labor. Each family was broken into five groups according to age. Each interview package was constructed on the following basis: The head of the household would have the Cornell Medical Index, the Life Change Survey, the Self-Anchoring Scale, the Peering Rating Scale, Demographic Interview (for household heads only), and Demographic Interview II (for all members age sixteen and over). The rest of the family members, if over twenty years old, would be given a packet consisting of CMI, LCS, SAS, PRS, and Demographic Interview II. Anyone between the ages of nineteen and thirteen would given the CMI, LCS, SAS, PRS, Social Prediction Scale I (for thirteen to nineteen years old only). Anyone seven to twelve years old would be given the SPS II (for seven-twelve years old only) and the Children's Manifest Anxiety Scale (CMAS). Finally, all family members twelve years old and over were given a physical examination.

Chronology of Events

1975

**April 8
through
April 15**
State Department officials consult with House and Senate Committees regarding use of Attorney General's "parole" authority for evacuees from Indochina.

April 12
U. S. Embassy, Phnom Penh closes. Last Americans are evacuated in operation "Eagle Pull."

**April 12
through
April 17**
U.S. Mission, Geneva asked to request assistance from United Nations High Commissioner for Refugees (UN-HCR) and Intergovernmental Committee for European Migration (ICEM) in locating third countries willing to accept refugees from Indochina.

April 14
Parole is authorized for dependents of American citizens currently in Vietnam.

April 18
The President asks twelve Federal agencies "to coordinate . . . all U. S. Government activities concerning evacuation of U. S. citizens, Vietnamese citizens, and third country nationals from Vietnam and refugee and resettlement problems relating to the Vietnam conflict" and names Ambassador L. Dean Brown as his Special Representative and Director of the Special Interagency Task Force.

April 19
Parole is extended to include categories of relatives of American citizens or permanent resident aliens who are petition holders.

April 22   The Interagency Task Force asks civil and military authorities on Guam to prepare a safe haven estimated to be required for 90 days in order to provide care and maintenance for an estimated 50,000 refugees. The first to pass through the area arrive the following day.

April 25   The Attorney General authorizes parole for additional categories of relatives, Cambodians in third countries and up to 50,000 "high-risk" Vietnamese.

April 27   The Task Force requests all American missions overseas to take up the possible resettlement of refugees as a matter of urgency.

April 29   U. S. Embassy, Saigon, closes. Operation Frequent Wind removes last Americans and Vietnamese by helicopter from staging sites in Saigon. The sea-lift and self-evacuation continue. Camp Pendleton, California, opens as a refugee center prepared to care for 18,000 refugees.

May 2   Fort Chaffee, Arkansas, opens as a refugee reception center prepared to care for 24,000 refugees.

May 4   Eglin Air Force Base, Florida, opens as a refugee reception center prepared to accept 2,500 refugees (a figure later increased to 5,000).

May 5   Ambassador Brown and senior Task Force officials testify before the Senate Foreign Affairs Committee.

Ambassador Brown and senior Task Force officials testify before the House Appropriations Defense Subcommittee in connection with the Administration's request for $507 million to run the refugee program.

May 7   Ambassador Brown and senior Task Force officials testify before the Senate Judiciary Committee, the House International Relations Committee, and on May 8, the House Judiciary Committee.

May 22   Ambassador Brown and senior Task Force officials testify before the House Judiciary Subcommittee.

A House and Senate conference committee agrees on the language of the Indochina Migration and Refugee Assistance Act of 1975, appropriating $405 million for the Administration's refugee program.

May 24   The Act becomes PL 94-23 as the President signs it into law.

May 27   Ambassador Brown returns to his post at the Middle East Institute, and the President asks Mrs. Julia Vadala Taft, Deputy Assistant Secretary of Health, Education, and Welfare for Human Development, to act as Director of the Interagency Task Force until arrangements are completed for organizing the Government's efforts for the longer term.

May 28   A fourth Stateside reception center is opened at Fort Indiantown Gap, Pennsylvania, and receives its first refugees.

May 29   The UNHCR sends a representative to Stateside reception center (Fort Chaffee) to interview individuals who have indicated a desire to return to Vietnam and whose names had been furnished earlier. Representatives of the UNHCR who have been working similarly on Guam for several weeks will go to Pendleton and Indiantown Gap next week and to Eglin thereafter.

June 6   HEW establishes a special Task Force with representatives of the American Medical Association, the American Association of Medical Colleges, the Educational Commission on Foreign Medical Graduates, and a number of programs within HEW that deal with training and placement of physicians in the U.S.

June 15   The President sends a Report to the Congress as required by PL 94-23.

July 5   First of a series of regional meetings with local government officials and representatives of resettlement agencies held in New York City.

July 6   Subic Bay, Philippines, refugee reception center closes.

July 21   Principal operational responsibility for the Task Force is transferred from the Department of State to the Department of Health, Education, and Welfare. Julia Vadala Taft is named as Director of the Task Force.

August 1   Wake Island reception center closes.

            Attorney General extends parole authority to additional Indochina refugees stranded in "third countries."

Sept. 15   Eglin Air Force Base, Florida, refugee reception center closes.

Sept. 23   The President transmits the Second Report to the Congress on the activities of the Interagency Task Force.

Sept. 30   Decision made to accede to demands of repatriates on Guam for a ship to be sailed by them to Vietnam.

Oct. 16   The Vietnamese freighter, Vietnam Thuong Tin I, sails from Guam bound for Vietnam with 1,546 repatriates aboard.

Oct. 31   Last date for movement of Indochina refugees stranded in third countries into the U.S. refugee system. Henceforth, admission of refugees into the United States is the responsibility of the Department of State.

UN High Commissioner for Refugees meets with Task Force and State Department officials. UNHCR agrees to accept responsibility for Cambodian refugees who do not wish to accept sponsorship offers and desire to be repatriated.

Reception centers on Guam and at Camp Pendleton, California, close.

Dec. 15   Indiantown Gap Military Reservation, Pennsylvania, refugee reception center closes.

Dec. 20   Last 24 refugees leave Fort Chaffee resettlement center to join sponsors, and this center, the last to remain in operation, is officially closed.

Dec. 31   Interagency Task Force operations are terminated, ending first phase of refugee program—evacuation and resettlement.

1976

Jan. 1   HEW Refugee Task Force assumes responsibility for domestic resettlement.

Feb. 6   State Department and Attorney General's office consult with Judiciary Subcommittee on Immigration, Citizenship, and International Law (Joshua Eilberg, Chairman) on issuance of parole authority to admit to the U.S. 11,000 Indochina refugees now in camps in Thailand.

Feb. 12   HEW Refugee Task Force and voluntary resettlement agencies (VOLAGs) meet in Washington to examine methods for a coordinated effort to assure opportunities for self-sufficiency among the new immigrants.

Feb. 18-19   Conference for HEW Regional Refugee Assistance Coordinators held in Washington to discuss domestic resettlement priorities.

Feb. 23-26   HEW Refugee Task Force Director and Deputy Regional Director attend a series of meetings with State of California, local county officials, and a number of VOLAG executive directors to discuss refugee resettlement issues.

March 15   Voluntary Agency directors sign HEW Strategy and Objectives Memorandum pledging to reduce cash assistance cases by 50 percent by October 1, 1976.

March 17   House Subcommittee on HEW Appropriation meets with HEW Refugee Task Force Director to discuss FY 1977 budget.

                 HEW Social and Rehabilitation Service establishes with the States a reporting system for Alien Registration Numbers of refugees on welfare.

March 31   Seattle regional conference of HEW Task Force, voluntary agencies, State officials, refugees, and sponsors yields guidelines for joint actions.

April 8   Senate Subcommittee on HEW Appropriations holds hearing on FY 1977 Refugee Task Force funding.

April 9   HEW Regional Offices are directed to develop plans for using seed monies to fund local activities designed to remove refugees from the cash assistance rolls and place them in jobs.

May 5   An Expanded Parole Program for 11,000 additional Cambodian, Vietnamese, and Laotian refugees is authorized by the Attorney General.

May 20-21   Representatives from HEW's Refugee Task Force, Office of Education, and Social and Rehabilitation Service (SRS) meet to develop Federal strategies on refugee assistance for the future, including the role of Indochinese self-help groups, and on the phasing of residual Task Force responsibilities into SRS.

June 4   Nationwide conference for State resettlement groups and representatives from State Governors' offices is held in Kansas City to exchange information and ideas.

$2 million allocated to the State of California for a special English language and vocational training program.

$400,000 allotted to Regional Offices to develop and implement job development programs for refugees.

June 23   New contract set up with Center for Applied Linguistics to continue toll-free phone service until 1977 and also to develop material and conduct training sessions in area of adult vocationally oriented English language training.

June 29   Contract with the American Bar Association, Young Lawyers Section, expanded to extend toll-free phone service for legal advice to refugees until March 1977. Also added were funds for ABA to research major legal problem areas being faced by refugees.

July 1   Laotians became eligible by P.L. 94-313 for benefits bestowed by Indochina Migration and Refugee Assistance Act of 1975 on Vietnamese and Cambodians.

July 12   Indochinese Mutual Assistance Division set up within HEW Refugee Task Force to provide technical assistance and liaison channels for more than 100 identified refugee self-help associations throughout the country.

July 14   Money allotted to Regional Offices to develop Mental Health Program for refugees.

July 21   Conference on cash assistance eligibility requirements for refugees. Participants included representatives from HEW, VOLAGs, state and local welfare agencies.

July 26   Notice of $5 million employment/training grant availability published in Federal Register.

July 26-30   Task Force visits to Regional Offices concerning $5 million employment/training grants to Regional staffs.

August 4   Draft of new cash assistance policy statement mailed to appropriate groups.

August 31   Applications for employment/training grants received in Regional Offices.

Sept. 10	Indochina Refugee Children Assistance Act of 1976 :P.L. 94-405) extending educational assistance for elementary-secondary students and adults for school year 1976-77.
Sept. 20	Third Wave Survey Report on Refugee Resettlement by Opportunity Systems Inc. completed.
Sept. 29	Administrator of Social and Rehabilitation Service, Commissioner of Assistance Payments Administration, and other SRS officials meet with national VOLAG Directors in preparation for transfer of Task Force responsibilities to SRS.
Sept. 30	SRS Regional Commissioners approve 58 grants totaling $5 million for English language and vocational training and job development and placement.
Oct. 1	HEW Indochina Refugee Task Force transferred from Office of the Secretary to Social and Rehabilitation Service, Assistance Payments Administration, U. S. Repatriate and Refugee Assistance Staff.
	Foreign Assistance and Related Programs Appropriation Act (P.L. 94-441) appropriated the remaining $50 million of the $455 million originally authorized by the Indochina Migration and Refugee Assistance Act of 1975. It also extended the availability to HEW of all appropriated funds until September 30, 1977.
Oct. 22	SRS Action Transmittal to the States providing revised guidelines for cash assistance for refugees, requiring acceptance of appropriate employment or training, and authorizing State welfare agencies to carry out job development activities.
Nov. 10	Completion by Task Force of initial Regional technical-assistance workshops for all employment/training project grantees.
Dec. 6	Contract awarded to Center for Applied Linguistics to provide technical assistance to employment program grantees.
Feb. 8	Completion by Task Force of second round of Regional assistance workshops for all employment/training project grantees.
May 4	Supplemental Appropriations Act (P.L. 95-26) includes

$18.5 million for funds to State educational agencies to reimburse local educational agencies for services to Indochinese refugee schoolchildren and $10.25 million for discretionary project grants to State and local educational agencies for English and vocational/occupational training for adult refugees. Funds were appropriated under authority of the Indochina Refugee Children Assistance Act of 1976 (P.L. 94-405).

Refugee Profile

Table 1

Indochina Refugees in the United States

June 1, 1977

Resettled under Special Parole Program   129,792

Resettled under Humanitarian Parole Program   500

Resettled under Special Lao Program   3,466

Resettled under Expanded Parole Program   11,000

Resettled under "Boat Cases" Program   150
                                                 _____

         Total in U.S. as of June 1, 1977   144,908 (*)

(*) There are 440 requests for repatriation before the UN High
     Commissioner for Refugees.

TABLE 2

Indochina Refugees in the United States

Rank	State	Number	Rank	State	Number
1	California	30,495	28	Nebraska	1,418
2	Texas	11,136	29	North Carolina	1,334
3	Pennsylvania	8,187	30	Connecticut	1,304
4	Virginia	5,620	31	Tennessee	1,250
5	Florida	5,237	32	Kentucky	1,174
6	Washington	5,205	33	New Mexico	1,047
7	New York	4,749	34	Utah	964
8	Illinois	4,675	35	South Carolina	926
9	Minnesota	4,250	36	Guam	818
10	Louisiana	3,916	37	Dist. of Columbia	613
11	Oklahoma	3,716	38	South Dakota	604
12	Ohio	3,496	39	Rhode Island	545
13	Iowa	3,352	40	Nevada	519
14	Missouri	3,154	41	Mississippi	493
15	Michigan	2,949	42	Idaho	421
16	Maryland	2,828	43	North Dakota	408
17	Wisconsin	2,461	44	Maine	376
18	Oregon	2,448	45	Montana	360
19	Hawaii	2,441	46	West Virginia	268
20	Colorado	2,350	47	Delaware	173
21	Indiana	2,175	48	New Hampshire	171
22	Arkansas	2,127	49	Wyoming	143
23	Kansas	1,953	50	Vermont	106
24	New Jersey	1,918	51	Alaska	94
25	Georgia	1,622	52	American Samoa	1
26	Arizona	1,444	52	Puerto Rico	1
27	Alabama	1,439			
28	Massachusetts	1,439		Totals:	

To Known State	142,283
To Unknown State	2,625
Grand Total	144,908

(Based on January 1976 INS Alien Address Reports projected to match Inter-Agency Task Force totals and the known destinations of those entering under the Special Lao & Expanded Parole Programs. A revised projection will be made upon availability of January 1977 INS data)

Table 3

ANALYSIS OF CASH ASSISTANCE CASE LOAD – INDOCHINA REFUGEES

	9/15/75	12/15/75	2/29/76	6/1/76	9/1/76	12/1/76	3/1/77	5/1/77
Number Resettled in U.S.	92,274	128,110	130,072	130,592	138,058	144,072	144,758	144,908
Cash Assistance Cases	3,362	8,705	11,854	13,688	14,205	14,955	16,856	17,684
Increase in Cases Since Previous Report	I/R	5,343	3,149	1,834	517	750	1,901	828
Percentage Increase in Cases since Previous	I/R	159%	36%	16%	4%	5%	13%	5%
Cash Assistance Persons	10,969	23,768	31,272	38,707	41,188	44,221	50,204	52,219
Increase in Persons Since Previous Report	I/R	12,799	7,504	7,518	2,481	3,033	5,983	2,015
Percentage Increase in Persons Since Previous	I/R	117%	32%	24%	6%	7%	14%	4%
Average number of persons Per Approved Case	3.26	2.44	2.63	2.82	2.89	2.96	2.98	2.95
Average Number of Persons Per New Case For Reporting Period	I/R	2.39	2.38	4.09	4.79	4.04	3.15	2.43
Percentage of Population on Cash Assistance	11.88%	18.55%	24.04%	29.63%	29.83%	30.69%	34.68%	36.04%

I/R = Initial Report

193

TABLE 4

Cash Assistance Cases - Indochina Refugees - By State

State	Number of Cases on Cash Assistance March 1, 1977	Number of Cases on Cash Assistance May 1, 1977	Percent Increase or Decrease
Region I			
Connecticut	115	117	+ 1.7%
Maine	15	16	+ 6.7%
Massachusetts	190	209	+10.0%
New Hampshire	15	14	- 6.7%
Rhode Island	40	53	+32.5%
Vermont	4	4	0
	379	413	+ 9.0%
Region II			
New York	226	238	+ 5.3%
New Jersey	148	143	- 3.4
Puerto Rico	0	0	0
Virgin Islands	0	0	0
	374	381	+ 1.9%
Region III			
Delaware	15	15	0%
Maryland	375	390	+ 4.0
Pennsylvania	604	662	+ 9.6
Virginia	591	622	+ 5.2
West Virginia	16	17	+ 6.3
Dist. of Columbia	141	114	-19.1
	1,742	1,820	+ 4.5%
Region IV			
Alabama	54	54	0%
Florida	520	561	+ 7.9
Georgia	69	67	- 2.9
Kentucky	152	127	-16.4
Mississippi	13	18	+38.5
North Carolina	97	90	- 7.2
South Carolina	24	28	+16.7
Tennessee	58	53	- 8.6
	987	998	+ 1.1%
Region V			
Illinois	394 [1]	368	- 6.6%
Indiana	148	137	- 7.4
Michigan	318 [1]	358	+12.6
Minnesota	282	287	+ 1.8
Ohio	287	290	+ 1.0
Wisconsin	230 [1]	247	+ 7.4
	1,659	1,687	+ 1.7%

1 Estimated

TABLE 4 (Continued)

Cash Assistance Cases – Indochina Refugees – By State

State	Number of Cases on Cash Assistance March 1, 1977	Number of Cases on Cash Assistance May 1, 1977	Percentage Increase or Decrease
Region VI			
Arkansas	92	103	+12.0%
Louisiana	292	326	+11.6%
New Mexico	17	24	+41.2%
Oklahoma	229	236	+ 3.1%
Texas	777	749	- 3.6%
	1,407	1,438	+ 2.2%
Region VII			
Iowa	305	285	- 6.6%
Kansas	113	125	+10.6%
Missouri	283	288	+ 1.8%
Nebraska	118	116	- 1.7%
	819	814	- 0.6%
Region VIII			
Colorado	386	333	-13.7%
Montana	51	49	- 3.9%
North Dakota	20	22	+10.0%
South Dakota	27	27	0
Utah	97	95	- 2.1%
Wyoming	4	3	-25.0%
	585	529	- 9.6%
Region IX			
Arizona	15	14	- 6.7%
California	6,250	7,000	+12.0%
Hawaii	603	610	+ 1.2%
Nevada	40	50	+25.0%
Guam	131	125	- 4.6%
Samoa	0	0	0 %
	7,039	7,799	+10.8%
Region X			
Alaska	0	2	- -
Idaho	21	25	+19.0%
Oregon	740	661	-10.7%
Washington	1,104	1,117	+ 1.2%
	1,865	1,805	- 3.2%
TOTAL	16,856	17,684	+ 4.9%

TABLE 5

WELFARE AND MEDICAL ASSISTANCE

FOR INDOCHINESE REFUGEES

(Reports from States as of May 1, 1977)

| States | Financial Assistance | | | | Medical Assistance (Only) | | |
| | Applications Authorized (Currently receiving) | | Applications Pending | | Authorized | Pending | |
	Cases	Persons	Cases	Persons	Persons	Cases	Persons
Alabama......	54	217	1	3	39	1	7
Alaska.......	2	2	0	0	0	0	0
Arizona......	14	55	0	0	0	0	0
Arkansas.....	103	326	19	na	116	na	na
California...	7,000	19,300	270	na	7,300	210	na
Colorado.....	333	1,173	12	na	141	0	0
Connecticut..	117	245	na	na	229	na	na
Delaware.....	15	50	0	0	15	0	0
Dist. of Col.	114	147	2	2	111	0	0
Florida......	561	1,618	23	67	248	8	20
Georgia......	67	185	1	1	66	3	14
Hawaii.......	610	1,607	5	12	104	3	7
Idaho........	25	122	1	na	60	1	na
Illinois.....	368	1,246	9	19	285	10	35
Indiana......	137	551	4	21	181	0	0
Iowa.........	285	837	1	1	1,477	2	3
Kansas.......	125	451	na	na	273	na	na
Kentucky.....	127	429	2	2	39	0	0
Louisiana....	326	1,388	56	280	128	5	32
Maine........	16	90	na	na	0	na	na
Maryland.....	390	800	10	40	575	15	40
Massachusetts	209	454	8	23	261	7	14
Michigan.....	358	1,323	7	26	247	5	8
Minnesota....	287	1,008	6	na	581	21	na
Mississippi..	18	71	0	0	8	0	0
Missouri.....	288	1,326	na	na	259	na	na
Montana......	49	164	1	na	31	0	0
Nebraska.....	116	418	na	na	102	na	na
Nevada.......	50	159	0	0	15	0	0
New Hampshire	14	24	na	na	20	na	na

TABLE 5 (continued)

WELFARE AND MEDICAL ASSISTANCE

FOR INDOCHINESE REFUGEES

(Reports from States as of May 1, 1977)

	Financial Assistance				Medical Assistance		
	Applications Authorized		Applications Pending		Authorized	Pending	
	(Currently receiving)						
States	Cases	Persons	Cases	Persons	Persons	Cases	Persons
New Jersey....	143	575	0	0	73	0	0
New Mexico....	24	118	5	25	211	6	24
New York......	238	788	2	8	526	0	0
North Carolina	90	216	0	0	63	0	0
North Dakota..	22	111	0	0	52	1	3
Ohio..........	290	897	0	0	598	0	0
Oklahoma......	236	612	8	22	175	12	33
Oregon........	661	1,867	4	8	224	1	1
Pennsylvania..	662	1,960	15	39	647	21	65
Rhode Island..	53	265	1	1	120	3	10
South Carolina	28	93	3	11	33	0	0
South Dakota..	27	141	0	0	78	0	0
Tennessee.....	53	158	5	7	60	5	8
Texas.........	749	2,381	38	160	324	10	57
Utah..........	95	260	2	9	64	1	3
Vermont.......	4	7	na	na	3	na	na
Virginia....1/	622	1,657	49	129	457	23	37
Washington....	1,117	2,967	8	8	291	1	2
West Virginia.	17	40	0	0	18	0	0
Wisconsin.....	247	955	na	na	630	na	na
Wyoming.......	3	10	0	0	0	0	0
Guam..........	125	355	na	na	98	na	na
	17,684	52,219	578	924	17,656	357	423

1/ As of 3/31/77.

Table 6

Labor Force Participation of Refugees 16 Years and Older:

March–April 1977 Survey
Wave IV, Opportunities Systems, Inc.

Sex	Total	In Labor Force	Not in Labor Force
Total	100.0%	62.5	37.5
Male	100.0%	76.5	23.6
Female	100.0%	44.5	55.5

N = 1,686.   Male, 932; Female, 754.   Weighted percentages.

Table 7

Employment Status of Refugees 16 Years and Older:

March–April 1977   Survey
Wave IV, Opportunities Systems, Inc.

Sex	Total	Employed	Unemployed
Total	100.0%	92.1	7.9
Male	100.0%	94.6	5.3
Female	100.0%	86.4	13.6

N = 1,022.   Male, 704; Female, 318.   Weighted percentages.

Table 8

Demographic Data

The Immigration and Naturalization Service (INS) provided
information and reports on the Indochina Refugees from the
annual Alien Address Report (Form I-53) received from aliens
by the INS. The following demographic data was prepared
from 114,140 Alien Address Reports identified as Indochina
Refugees.

Distribution by Age and Sex

Based on 114,140 refugees, January 1976 INS Alien Report

AGE	MALE		FEMALE		TOTAL	
0 - 5	8,250	14.24 %	8,319	14.80%	16,569	14.52 %
6 - 11	8,485	14.65	8,269	14.71	16,754	14.68
12 - 17	7,824	13.51	7,487	13.32	15,311	13.41
18 - 24	11,364	19.62	9,476	16.85	20,840	18.26
25 - 34	10,612	18.32	10,212	18.16	20,824	18.25
35 - 44	5,481	9.46	5,115	9.10	10,596	9.28
45 - 62	4,046	6.99	4,175	7.43	8,221	7.20
63 & Over	1,857	3.21	3,168	5.63	5,025	4.40
TOTAL	57,919	100.00 %	56,221	100.00 %	114,140	100.00 %

MALES

17 and under	-	24,559	42.40 %
Over 17	-	33,360	57.60 %
TOTAL		57,919	100.00 %

FEMALES

17 and under	-	24,075	42.82 %
Over 17	-	32,146	57.18 %
TOTAL		56,221	100.00 %
Total Male Population	-	57,919	50.74 %
Total Female Population	-	56,221	49.26 %
Total Population	-	114,140	100.00 %

Voluntary Resettlement Agencies (VOLAGS)

	Approximate Number of Refugees Resettled
United States Catholic Conference Migration and Refugee Services 1312 Massachusetts Avenue, N.W. Washington, D.C. 20005 Telephone (202) 659-6635	60,000
International Rescue Committee 386 Park Avenue South New York, New York 10016 Telephone (212) 679-0010	19,500
Church World Service Immigration & Refugee Program 475 Riverside Drive New York, New York 10027 Telephone (212) 870-2164	19,000
Lutheran Immigration & Refugee Services 360 Park Avenue South New York, New York 10010 Telephone (212) 532-6350	18,500
HIAS, Inc. 200 Park Avenue South New York, New York 1003 Telephone (212) 674-6800	3,900

Tolstoy Foundation, Inc.
250 West 57th Street
New York, New York 10019
Telephone (212) 247-2922   3,600

American Council for
Nationalities Service
20 West 50th Street
New York, New York 10018
Telephone (21) 398-9142   4,830

American Fund for Czechoslovak
Refugees
1790 Broadway, Room 513
New York, New York 10019
Telephone (212) 265-1919   1,200

Travelers Aid International
Social Service of America
345 East 46th Street
New York, New York 10017
Telephone (212) 687-2747   530

State and Local Resettlement Agencies

Approximate Number of
Refugees Resettled

Department of Emergency Services
State of Washington
4220 East Martin Way
Olympia, Washington 98504
Telephone (206) 753-5255   1,732

Governor's Task Force for
Indo-Chinese Resettlement
Employment Security Commission
State of Iowa
1000 East Grand Avenue
Des Moines, Iowa 50319
Telephone (515) 281-5362   1,207

Department of Institutions,
Social and Rehabilitative Services
State of Oklahoma
Post Office Box 25352
Oklahoma City, Oklahoma 73125
Telephone (405) 521-3076   362

Division of Community Services
State of Maine
193 State Street
The State House
Augusta, Maine 04333
Telephone (207) 289-3771   167

Governor's Cabinet Secretariat
State of New Mexico Planning Office
403 Executive-Legislative Building
Santa Fe, New Mexico 87501
Telephone (505) 827-2112   545

Jackson County, Missouri
Don Bosco Community Center
526 Campbell Street
Kansas City, Missouri 64106
Telephone (816) 421-5825   386

City of Indianapolis
Indianapolis Chapter, American RedCross
441 East Tenth Street
Indianapolis, Indiana 46202
Telephone (317) 634-1441   80

Chinese Consolidated Benevolent
Association of Los Angeles
923-925 North Broadway
Los Angeles, California 90012
Telephone (213) 683-1950   838

Chinese Consolidated Benevolent
Association of New York
62 Mott Street
New York, New York 10013
Telephone (212) 539-5663   72

Church of Jesus Christ
of Latter Day Saints
50 East North Temple
Salt Lake City, Utah 84101
Telephone (801) 531-2531   700

DATE

ADP ID CARD
MCBCP-3305/4 (5-75)

CARD Ø			PLACE OF BIRTH	Noi sinh	CITY Tinh	COUNTRY Xu
71-79	AREA	VOLAG	TENT			
22-41	PASSPORT NO.					
1-7	GEN NUM	0039597				
42-56	VA CLAIM NO.					
8-13	FAMILY CONTROL NUM		57-65			
	P		66	MARITAL STATUS	Tinh Trang Gia Dinh	
14				M-Married	D-Divorced	S-Single
	NATIONALITY Quoc tich			co vo	ly di	doc than
15	V-VIET A-AMER E-CAMB O-OTHER		67-72	DATE OF ARRIVAL U.S. RECEPTION CENTER		
	STATUS Phan loai			Ngay toi trung-tam tiep-cu Hoa-ky		
16	A-REPAT Hoi-huong R-Refugee Ty-nan			YY MM DD		
17-46	NAME IN VIETNAMESE ORDER Ho-Ten		73-79	Ø 80 2		
47-56	MOTHER'S GIVEN NAME Ten nguoi me		CARD A	1-14 SAME		
	SEX.		15-16	DESIRED RELOCATION AREA BY STATE CODE		
57	M-Dan ong F-Dan ba			Noi muon xin dinh-cu		
58-63	DOB Ngay sinh YY MM DD		17	IMMIGRATION STATUS Tinh-trang cu-tru		
64-70	GUAM CONT NUM So kiem soat tai GUAM			P-PAROLEE R-U.S. RESIDENT Q-PENDING		
80	Ø		18	WHO WORKED FOR IN INDOCHINA		
CARD I	1-14 SAME			1-EMBASSY 3-DAO 5-OTHER		
				2-AID 4-VIETNAM GOV 6-NONE		
15-17	SIZE OF FAMILY Gia-dinh may nguoi		19-24	DATE OF ENTRY ON DUTY		
	LAST RESIDENCE CITY COUNTRY			YY MM DD		
18-34	Dia-chi cuoi cung o VN Tinh Xu		25	D-DIRECT HIRE C-CONTRACT		
			26-35	MISSION ID CARD NO.		
			36-38	GRADE FSL ETC.		
				POSITION (CLEAR TEXT)		

41	G-GUAM W-WAKE S-SUBIC C-CLARK M-BY SEA
42-47	DATE OF DEPARTURE LAST PROCESS CENTER Ngay roi di YY MM DD
48-59	PRIMARY JOB SKILL (CLEAR TEXT) Nghe chuyen mon chanh
60-62	JOB CODE
63-73	SECONDARY JOB SKILL (CLEAR TEXT) Nghe chuyen-mon phu
74-76	JOB CODE
77	COUNTRY OF BIRTH Sanh quan V-VIET A-AMER C-CAMB
78	HEAD OF HOUSEHOLD Chu gia-dinh Y-YES N-NO
79	RELIGION Ton giao B-BUDDIST P-PROT C-CATH O-OTHER Phat Tinlanh Conggiao
80	|

CARD 2

15	CATEGORY OF INDIVIDUAL G-VIET CIVIL SERV O-OFFICER (MIL) E-ENLISTED Y-OTHER
16	EDUCATION E-ELEMENTARY S-SECONDARY U-UNIVERSITY P-POST GRAD
17	LANGUAGE S-SOME G-GOOD N-NATIVE FR 18 ENG 19 V 20 C
21	EVACUEE FAMILY MEMBER MISSING Gia-dinh co guoi bi that-lac khong? Y-YES N-NO

CARD 3   1-14 SAME

15-20	DATE OF MEDICAL EXAM YY MM DD
21	MEDICAL STATUS G-GOOD T-TEMP DISB P-PERM DISB
22	HOSPITALIZED Y-YES N-NO
23-28	DATE OF HOSPITALIZATION YY MM DD
29-48	REASON FOR HOSPITALIZATION (CLEAR TEXT)
49-54	DATE OF DISCHARGE FROM HOSPITAL YY MM DD
55	X-RAY RESULTS P-POSITIVE N-NEGATIVE
56	SEROLOGY P-POSITIVE N-NEGATIVE
57	FINAL MEDICAL CLEARANCE Y-YES N-NO

PPD - MM

						NOT READ			
DPT DATES	1	2	3	B	POLIO	1	2	3	B
MMR DATE	DT								

58-79	COMMENTS - REASON FOR NO CLEARANCE (CLEAR TEXT)
80	3

ADP ID CARD
MCBCP-3305/4 (5-75) BACK

CENTRAL PROCESSING

CARD 4

Position	Field
1-7	GEN NUM
8-13	FAMILY CONTROL NUM
14	P
15-22	ALIEN NO.
23-31	SSN
32-37	DATE OF CENTRAL PROCESSING YY MM DD
38-47	PROCESSING ORGANIZATION
48-57	CONVERTIBLE CASH RESOURCES $
58-67	OTHER RESOURCES $
68	RELATIVES RESIDING IN U.S. Y-YES N-NO
69	FRIENDS RESIDING IN U.S. Y-YES N-NO
70	SPONSORSHIP INDICATOR N-NONE P-POTENTIAL V-VERIFIED
71-79	ORGANIZATION VERIFYING SPONSORSHIP
80	4

CARD 5   1-14 SAME

FINAL PROCESSING (Continued)

CARD 8   1-14 SAME

Position	Field
15-20	DATE OF RELEASE FROM REFUGEE CAMP YY MM DD
21-55	STREET ADDRESS OF DESTINATION
56-72	CITY
73-74	STATE CODE
75-79	ZIP CODE
80	8

CARD 9   1-14 SAME

Position	Field
15-18	MEDICAL EXPENDITURE BY HEW $
19-22	SPENDING MONEY GIVEN BY HEW $
23-26	TRANSPORTATION MONEY GIVEN BY HEW $
27-30	OTHER EXPENDITURE GIVEN BY HEW $
31-49	REASON FOR OTHER EXPENDITURE
50	REPAYMENT I-INFULL S-INSTALLMENT W-WAIVER
51-56	DATE 1ST INSTALLMENT PAYMENT DUE YY MM DD
57-79	COMMENTS

AFFIDAVIT OR I-134 FORM COMPLETED

16	Y-YES N-NO
17	IS SPONSOR RELATED Y-YES N-NO
18-37	NAME OF SPONSOR
38-79	ADDRESS OF SPONSOR (STREET)
80	5

| 80 | 9 |

CARD 6   1-14 SAME

15-32	RESIDENCE OF SPONSOR CITY
33-34	STATE CODE
35-39	ZIP CODE

FINAL PROCESSING

40	HAS SPONSOR Y-YES N-NO P-POTENTIAL
41	HAS FUNDS FOR TRAVEL Y-YES N-NO S-SPONSOR WILL PROVIDE
42	INS CLEARANCE COMPLETED Y-YES N-NO
43	MEDICAL CLEARANCE COMPLETE Y-YES N-NO
44-79	DISPOSITION COMMENTS

FINAL CLEARANCE

| SSA | ADP |
| SRS | INS |

CAMP COMMANDER

| 80 | 6 |

TELEPHONE NO. OF SPONSOR

References Cited

Cantril, Hadley
    1965   *The Pattern of Human Concerns*, New Brunswick: Rutgers University Press, 1965

Chuman, Dwight
    1975   "Camp Pendleton Refugee Experience," *RAFU Shimpo:* Los Angeles Japanese Daily News, May 22, 1975

Harding, Richard K. and John G. Looney
    1977   "Problems of Southeast Asian Children in a Refugee Camp," *American Journal of Psychiatry*, 134:407-411

Harris, Louis
    1975   "Harris Survey, Refugees' Lukewarm Reception," *Chicago Tribune*

Harrison, Donald
    1975   "The Refugees from Vietnam," *San Diego Union*, May 1-2

Heider, F.
    1958   *The Psychology of Interpersonal Relationships*, New York: John Wiley

Holborn, Louise
    1968   "Refugees," *Encyclopaedia of the Social Sciences*, Vol. 13:361

Kneeland, D. E.
    1975a "Many Refugees Are Reluctant to Leave the Security of Four Camps and Get Resettled," *New York Times*, July 22
    1975b "Resettlement Nearing But Not Refugee Problems," *New York Times*, November 24

Kuepper, Lackey and others
    1974   *The Uganda Refugees in London*, unpublished

Kunz, E. F.
  1973   "The Refugee in Flight: Kinetic Models and Forms of Displacement," *International Migration Review*, 7:125-146
Liang, R. A.
  1969   *The Politics of the Family*, New York: Random House
Looney, J. G.
  1975a   "Consultation Report: Psychiatric Problems of the Children and Adolescents of the Vietnamese and Cambodian Refugee Population," *United States Naval Health Research Center Report*, May 20
  1975b   "Consultation Paper" *United States Naval Health Research Center Report*, July 7
  1975c   "Memorandum to Captain J. J. Gunning," July 31
Lyon, Jeff
  1975   "Many Viet Refugees on Aid Despite U. S. Cash," *Chicago Tribune* December 8
Milwaukee Journal
  1975   "Viet Refugees on North Side, Elsewhere, Need Federal Aid," September 28
Mineta, Norman Y., Leslie Francis, Patricia Ginger, and Larry Low
  1975   *Southeast Asian Refugee Evacuation and Resettlement Program*, Washington, D.C. *mineo.*
Murphy, J. M., Murfin G., D. and N. L. Jamieson
  1974   "Beliefs, Attitudes and Behavior of Lowland Vietnamese, Part B. The Effects of Herbicides in South Vietnam," Washington, D.C.: The National Academy of Science
New York Times
  1975   Articles on refugees on May 21, April 25, July 22, and November 24
Newsweek
  1975   Report on Vietnamese refugees in the following issues: May 5, 12, 19 and 26
Rahe, Richard H., and E. Lind
  1971   "Psychosocial Factors and Sudden Cardiac Death: A Pilot Study," *Journal of Psychosomatic Research*, 15:19-24
Rahe, Richard H., I. Floistad, T. Bergen, *et al.*
  1974   "A Model for Life Changes and Illness Research," *Archive of General Psychiatry*, 31:172-177
Rahe, Richard H., M. Romo and L. Bennett, *et al.*
  1974   "Recent Life Changes, Myocardial Infarction, and Abrupt Coronary Death," *Archive of Internal Medicine*, 133:221-228
Rahe, Richard
  1975a   "Memo to Captain J. J. Gunning on Consultation on Psychiatric and Social Problems of Vietnamese Evacuees at Camp Pendleton," May 20

1975b   "Memo to Captain J. J. Gunning," July 25

1975c   (with J. G. Looney) "Memo to Captain J. J. Gunning, on Psychiatric Status of Unaccompanied Vietnamese Children"

1975d   "Epidemiological Studies of Life Change and Illness," *International Journal of Psychiatric Medicine*, 6:133-146

1972   "Subjects' Recent Life Changes and Their Near-future Illness Report," *Ann Clinical Research*, 4:250-265

Rotter, J. B.,

1966   "Generalized Expectations for Internal vs. External Control of Reinforcement," *Psychological Monographs*, No. 609

Segal, Julius, and Norman Lourie

1975   "Memo to Rear Adm. G. Morrison: The Mental Health of the Vietnamese Refugees," unpublished

Scott, Austin

1975   "Refugee Camp Winds Up: Fort Chaffee Having Few Problems with Resettlement," *Washington Post*, September 14

Shaw, R.

1977   "Preventive Medicine in the Vietnamese Refugee Camps on Guam," *Milit Med* 142:19-28

Sussman, Lesley

1975   "Refugees Fear Discontent of Winter," *Milwaukee Journal*, Sept. 28

Thibaut, J., and H. H. Kelley

1959   *The Social Psychology of Groups*, New York: John Wiley

Thibaut, J. W., and H. W. Riesken

1955   "Some Determinants and Consequences of the Perception of Social Causality," *J. Pors*, 24:113-133

Time, May 19, 1975

Tung, Tran Minh, M.D.

1975a   "Mental Health Trends in the Vietnamese Refugee Population as Seen in the Mental Health Clinic of Camp Pendleton (California)," Camp Pendleton, California, (Mimeo)

1975b   "The Vietnamese Refugees and Their Health Problems: A Vantage View." Paper presented at a meeting of Columbia Chapter in Washington Psychiatric Society and of the Medical Society of the District of Columbia, Washington, D. C., October 1

Tuyet, Nguyen Anh

1975   "Some Refugees Fleeing Sponsors," *Washington Post*, August 26

United Nations, 1979. *Refugee Report*

U. S. Department H.E.W.

1975   "Information About the Indochina Refugee Resettlement Program," San Francisco: AA, (Mimeo)

U. S. Interagency Task Force for Indochina Refugees (IATF)

1975a "First Wave Report: Vietnam Resettlement Operational Feedback," Washington, D.C., (Mimeo)

1975b "Report to the Congress," Washington, D.C., (Mimeo)

U. S. Marine Corps

1975 "Operation New Arrivals: After Action Report," Camp Pendleton, Los Angeles, (Mimeo)

U. S. News and World Report, May 8, 1975, May 19, 1975

Weston, W.D.

1975 "Development of Community Psychiatry Concepts," in *Comprehensive Textbook of Psychiatry II.* Edited by Freeman A.M., Kaplan H.I., Sadock B.J., Baltimore: The Williams & Wilkins Company

Zigler, E.

1976 "A Developmental Psychologist's View of Operation Babylift" *American Psychologist,* May, 329-340

1897 0=